THE CHRISTIAN AND ANXIETY

HANS URS VON BALTHASAR

The Christian and Anxiety

Translated by Dennis D. Martin
and Michael J. Miller

With a Foreword by
Yves Tourenne, O.F.M.
translated from the second
French edition by Adrian Walker

IGNATIUS PRESS   SAN FRANCISCO

Originally published as *Der Christ und die Angst* (1952)
Reissued in the series "Christ heute", 2d series, volume 3
© 1989 Johannes Verlag, Einsiedeln, Trier

Foreword by Yves Tourenne, O.F.M.,
taken from the 2d French edition,
Le Chrétien et l'angoisse
© 1994 Desclée de Brouwer, Paris
Translated and used by permission

Cover design by Roxanne Mei Lum

© 2000 Ignatius Press, San Francisco
All rights reserved
ISBN 0-89870-587-8
Library of Congress catalogue number 96-83637
Printed in the United States of America ∞

CONTENTS

FOREWORD TO THE
SIXTH GERMAN EDITION
(1989)

In response to many requests from our readers, we venture to issue this small book again, shortly after the death of its author.

"Following upon philosophical and psychological studies of the topic, this is the first strictly theological study of anxiety. Taking Sacred Scripture as its point of departure, it seeks to grasp the general Christian laws that determine the meaning and limits of anxiety, so as to establish finally its essence in a speculative way." That is how the book was introduced to its readers in 1953. Since that time, through a lively exchange with the steadily advancing insights and observations of psychology and psychiatry, anxiety has become a burning issue in theology as well. The author had intended to complete his earlier work by incorporating into it the fruits of this interdisciplinary dialogue. It was a great disappointment for many that he did not have the opportunity to do so. The theological foundation that is laid in this first study, though, may well continue to stimulate further work.

TRANSLATOR'S NOTE

Angst has entered into the English language on a popular level, usually conveying psychological overtones. Although neither "anxiety" nor "anguish", "insecurity" nor "fear" by itself fully captures the range of connotations of the German word, "anxiety" and "anguish" have generally been employed for direct translation of *Angst*. Since the entire book seeks to explain the range of meanings of *Angst*, it seems unlikely that the richness and variety of "anxiety" will be lost on the reader.

Depending on the context, *Geist* in German can mean "mind", "ghost" or "spirit". In this book, which is a response to Kierkegaard's analysis of anxiety and the repercussions that it had in German Catholic and Lutheran theology, the term is used in contradistinction to *Seele*, "soul", and often denotes the human faculty of "intellect" in the Aristotelian sense. Therefore *Geist* has been translated as "mind" (cf. *Geistesgeschichte*, intellectual history).

Unless otherwise noted, Scripture quotations have been taken from the Revised Standard Version, Catholic edition.

Michael J. Miller

FOREWORD

A Theology of Anxiety?

The Christian and Anxiety[1] is a demanding book. Its dense philosophical analyses, its frequent dramatic passages, and its commentaries on numerous biblical texts can easily deter the prospective reader. In order to glimpse the greatness of Hans Urs von Balthasar's work through this thicket of difficulties, we need to get a good handle on the method he adopts in it.

Balthasar never separates method from content. The object itself entails a certain way of conceiving and approaching it, just as method is already a matter of content. That having been said, it is nonetheless good to distinguish the two levels.

An outline of the book helps to bring its method into relief. The work opens with a reflection on the Bible; at the beginning of chapter 2, Balthasar tells us that, throughout the remainder of the discussion, we must keep in mind what the Word of God alone (*CA*, 81ff.) is able to teach us about anxiety [*angst*]. The first, scriptural part of the book is meant to portray both the contemporary situation and the then current accounts of anxiety, Freudian or philosophical. Although the introduction reflects the situation of the time in which

[1] Henceforth abbreviated as *CA* in references.

the book was written, Balthasar insists (*CA*, 35) on
the need to take distance from it, lest the analysis of
anxiety prove to be yet another expression of it.

The reader should approach the second chapter of
the work, which could be called its center (it has the
same title as the book), only in terms of the first. Yet
even when he does so, he will encounter certain sur-
prisingly abrupt statements. These statements can be
accounted for by the fact that it is the Word of *God*
that puts human anxiety (of which the Christian is at
once the victim—like every man—and the conqueror)
in its proper perspective. Balthasar's method, which
makes the Word of God both the starting point and
the permanent basis of reflection, may be reminiscent
of Karl Barth's "verticalism". In truth, Balthasar shows
that the necessary *distance* mentioned above, by a kind
of *incidental* side effect (*CA*, 36), results in a capacity
to go to the very heart of contemporary anxiety.

For this reason, *The Christian and Anxiety* ends with
a third part, which initially can be described as philosophical. The Catholic thinker cannot remain content
with a kind of *sola scriptura* or even with a purely theological account of anxiety. If theology is going to reach
contemporary man, it has to integrate philosophical reflection.

Balthasar thus proceeds to link philosophy and theology.[2] This link has a twofold basis. On the one hand,

---

[2] Balthasar consistently refused a theology dissociated from contem-

revelation takes account of the anthropological phenomenon of anxiety.[3] On the other hand, philosophy,
at least in the modern period (Hegel, Kierkegaard,
Heidegger, Sartre), has seen anxiety as a fundamental dimension of man's existence (*CA*, 119). Hence
Balthasar's search for a point of contact, an intrinsic link, between reflection on revelation and reflection on human existence. The object of philosophy is
always more than philosophical (*CA*, 115); it stands
out against an original horizon, as Merleau-Ponty and
Lévinas, following Husserl, have shown. From the
Catholic point of view, the concrete world on which
philosophy reflects is never a pure *natura* but is always
the world that is sustained and penetrated by grace.
Theology, for its part, precisely because it reflects on
God's self-revelation in man's history and speech (Israel, Jesus, the Church), necessarily entails ontological
reflection: revelation meets and illuminates man's situation in the world at an undreamed-of depth.

In this way, Balthasar the theologian, speaking as he
does to the men of his time, quite naturally picks up

---

plative prayer (cf. Il discorso di Hans Urs von Balthasar. In: *Hans Urs
von Balthasar, Premio Internazionale Paolo VI* [Brescia: Instituto Paolo
VI, 1984] 27–28), on the one hand, and a theology not intimately
connected with philosophy (cf. *The Glory of the Lord: A Theological
Aesthetics*, vol. 1: *Seeing the Form* [San Francisco: Ignatius Press, 1982],
143–47), on the other. According to Balthasar, the Renaissance and
the Reformation conspired to consummate this double dissociation.

[3] *CA*, 39 ("Das Wort Gottes kennt keine Angst vor der Angst").

themes and accents of contemporary thought: Kierkegaard, Heidegger, existentialism. . . . We could therefore say, using Balthasar's own terminology, that there
is both a distance and a mutual reflection [*ricochet*] between attentive listening to revelation (chapter 1) and
ontological reflection (chapter 3).

Finally, Balthasar goes on to forge an original account of the link between the Old and New Tes-
taments. Although both together make up the one
revelation,[4] a profound transformation occurs in the
passage from the former to the latter. The New Testament marks a break; it radically intensifies the revelation of anxiety. At Gethsemani and on the Cross, all
possible anxiety, both of the just and of the guilty, is
concentrated upon the Redeemer—and this very con-
centration is the absolute revelation of grace, the eschatological gift of peace, the victory, at once promised
and already granted, over all anxiety (*CA*, 81ff.).

Man's Anxiety, God's Anxiety [5]

The purpose of Balthasar's method is to legitimate the
work's central project of giving a Christian interpretation of anxiety, or rather, of clearing a path to the
root meaning of anxiety by refusing to take what is

---

[4] Cf. *CA*, 36: "a comprehensive perspective".

[5] *CA*, 81ff. and 73; cf. 146.

just one of its manifestations—the morbidity of our time—as its ultimate meaning (*CA*, 36).

The Christian and Anxiety centers on an elucidation of man's anxiety in the light of Christ and the Trinity. Anxiety, with its emptiness and darkness, with its entanglement in sin (which is more than just man's finitude), is redeemed. Anxiety finds its ultimate meaning in the fact that the Word of God has taken it upon himself. Anxiety thus has a *christological* meaning, which concerns nothing less than the authenticity of God's incarnation in Jesus as defined by Chalcedon (451), Lateran I (649), and Constantinople III (681). For his part, Balthasar writes that "God could not become man in any other way than by coming to know human fear and by taking it upon himself" (*CA*, 74).

But the christological meaning of anxiety reveals in turn the mystery of the *Trinity*. The Word of God made flesh discloses the divine secrets: "In standing outside [*Hinausstehen*] of eternity and entering into time, the Son of Man has known anxiety and therein, as in everything he was, did, and suffered, he has translated something incomprehensible and divine into human language (that is, after all, what revelation is): God's fear and trembling [*Bangen und Beben*] for the world, for his creation, which is on the verge of being lost" (*CA*, 146; cf. 74).

The revelation of the Trinity in the economy of salvation opens a window onto an abyss at which Balthasar merely hints here but which he discusses more amply in later works:[6] the infinite distance between the Persons within the eternal and indivisible Trinity. It is this distance that grounds the possibility of creation, history, the drama of redemption, and the believer's leap [*saut*] of faith, hope, and charity. If man experiences anxiety as a void, the possibility of this void lies in "the everlasting trinitarian ecstasy".[7]

This Christology and trinitarian theology underlie the *soteriological* meaning of anxiety. *The Christian and Anxiety* contains reflections on one of the key themes in Balthasar's work: substitution [*Stellvertretung*]. The whole of human anxiety, concentrated in a single mass, closes in upon Christ, who alone can say Yes to God the Father in place of the sinner's resolute No. But this act is the condition upon which the fulfillment of God's saving plan depends. Human anxiety thus becomes the material, as it were, by which Jesus restores the fallen creation to his Father and imparts to it God's absolution. Balthasar thus resists any tendency to wallow in, or consent to, morbid anxiety; "adamantly and trenchantly" (*CA*, 88), he reminds us that Christ admonishes his disciples against anxiety.

[6] In *Theo-Drama: Theological Dramatic Theory*, vol. 4: *The Action* (San Francisco: Ignatius Press, 1994), and vol. 5: *The Last Act* (San Francisco: Ignatius Press, 1998), 91–95.

[7] CA, 148; cf. 145. See also *Theo-Drama*, 4:319–20, on the absolute distance between the Persons in the eternal Trinity and their "primal drama"; *Theo-Drama*, 5:81–84. See also *Mysterium Paschale* (Grand Rapids: Eerdmans, 1990).

Turning from the Bible and theology, Balthasar goes on to examine the nature or essence [*das Wesen*] of anxiety by means of a *philosophical* analysis that builds on Kierkegaard and other contemporary thinkers.

Open Readings

Other writers, philosophers, and theologians appear throughout *The Christian and Anxiety*. A typically Balthasarian attitude is at work here. Himself a translator and publisher, Balthasar was a *reader*, and his own thought, while highly personal, always contains echoes of other intellectual systems, with which he maintains a living bond symbolized by the proper names he cites.[8]

One way to enter into Balthasar's thought process is to note the proper names he cites, to compile an index, and to try to understand why certain names appear in certain passages or alongside certain other names. Among such names, two seem to be particularly important for the present work: Kierkegaard and Bernanos.

Although Balthasar has a certain kinship with Kierkegaard, the author of *The Concept of Anxiety* (1844)

---

[8] Hence Balthasar's presentation of numerous authors, for example in the two volumes of *The Glory of the Lord* entitled *Studies in Theological Style*, *Clerical Styles* (vol. 2) and *Lay Styles* (vol. 3) (San Francisco: Ignatius Press, 1984 and 1986, respectively). For Balthasar, "true history is made up of the distillation of countless biographies", *Theo-Drama*, 3:282, n. 13.

also represents an option that Balthasar will reject: a purely psychological and philosophical analysis of anxiety inspired by German Idealism (which, however, Kierkegaard also criticizes) and Lutheran dogmatics (*CA*, 136–39). Bernanos, on the other hand, is a mine of invaluable characters and themes, which Balthasar aims to develop into a theology.

There are, however, discreet presences to which we must also be attentive. We note, for example, the name of Henri de Lubac (*CA*, 139–40), who, as is well known, was akin to Balthasar in spirit.[9] For Balthasar, anxiety, by its very nature, has to be understood within the paradox of the finite spirit,[10] whose acts of knowledge and freedom, while always focusing on some particular object, are open to the infinite. There is, it seems to me, a deep kinship between *The Christian and Anxiety*, especially in the last part of the book, and the work of de Lubac.[11]

We can also detect the even more discreet presence of Karl Rahner. Rahner is mentioned twice, each time

---

[9] A letter from Balthasar to de Lubac dating from July 1950 (printed in H. de Lubac, *Theology in History* [San Francisco: Ignatius Press, 1996], 597) reveals the friendship uniting the two theologians.

[10] Cf. *CA*, 123. An important term in de Lubac, likewise in Balthasar. On p. 150 he uses the expression "paradox of the Church", which is reminiscent of the title of one of de Lubac's later works: *Paradoxe et mystère de l'Eglise* (1967).

[11] Cf. H. de Lubac, *Surnaturel, Paradoxes*; cf. de Lubac's approach to anxiety, "whose psychological substitutes can never be sufficiently decried", in *Sur les chemins de Dieu* (Paris: Aubier, 1956), 212–13.

with the approbation with which one cites an author-
ity (*CA*, 113 and 124, n. 1). One also notes a certain affinity between the two thinkers when Balthasar,
in order to define the locus of anxiety, insists on the
"indispensable" (*CA*, 116) role of philosophy in theology and on the "reciprocal relationship" and "suspension" between transcendence and contingency in the
human mind.[12] Thus, despite their different theological
sensibilities, Balthasar and Rahner maintained a certain
closeness before their disagreement at the time of *The
Moment of Christian Witness* [*Cordula*] (1966) and the
fourth volume of *Theo-Drama* (1980).

From First Glance to Systematic Rereading

For those approaching the book for the first time,
The Christian and Anxiety is best read through once,
without lingering over any one part or passage. They

---

[12] Cf. *CA*, 124. "Reciprocal relationship" is a typically Rahner-
ian expression, at least from the time of the publication of *Geist
in Welt* in 1939 (to which Balthasar refers explicitly in the note on
page 124). In saying that man's cognition is structurally "suspended"
[*schwebend*] (*CA*, 126–27) between the two poles of being and the existent, Balthasar refers to a motif also present in Rahner (from *L'Esprit
dans le monde* [French trans. 1968], 72ff.; English trans.: *Spirit in the
World* [New York: Herder and Herder, 1968] to *Traite fondamental de
la foi* [French trans. 1983], 88ff.; English trans.: *Foundations of Christian Faith* [New York: Crossroad, 1970]), which he, Balthasar, had
already underscored in his 1939 review of *Geist in Welt* (in *Zeitschrift
für Katholische Theologie* [Innsbruck, 1939]: 378).

should try, in other words, to see the unity of the
work through the connection, and the tension, between its scriptural, theological, and ontological dimensions. Having done so, they can return to the text for
a rereading. I would like to suggest four points to look
for here.

*Balthasar lays down two principles, one negative and one
positive, concerning the nature of anxiety.* On the one hand,
the Christian neither can nor should have firsthand
knowledge of anxiety, for by his Passion and death
Christ has assumed and conquered it. On the other
hand, the Christian receives from Christ a participation in his redemptive anxiety.

These two assertions appear to be sharply contradic-
tory. In themselves, they are the elements that make up
Balthasar's specifically Christian and theological judgment on the situation of his time. From the introduction on (*CA*, 34ff.), Balthasar insists on the need for
a certain distance from the two false attitudes that the
above-mentioned principles are meant to counter: se-
duction by the morbid anxiety that surrounds us, on
the one hand, and "a serene theology of irrelevance",
on the other (*CA*, 35).

Balthasar's two theses are thus to be grasped like
the two ends of a chain. But there is still need for a
mediation between them. This mediation is joy, the
truly personal appropriation of the objective redemption. The Christian can be called to participate in the
anxiety of the Cross only because he has first received

grace. Genuine Christian anxiety is a function of joy and a gift of God. Balthasar concurs with Nietzsche, albeit for an entirely different reason: It is the strong who help the weak, it is the spiritually healthy who are compassionate, but without "a cringing Christianity's" (Bernanos, *CA*, 86–88) indulgence of contemporary anxiety.

This position also has implications for theology. Theology must not share in the ambiguities and darkness of its time, above all if it wants to be present to its contemporaries. Balthasar thus lays the theological groundwork for Christian anxiety, which, while being radically different from contemporary anxiety, refuses to distance itself pharisaically from it.[13]

"Catholic Anxiety"

"Catholic anxiety"—*this* is at the center of the book (*CA*, 92; cf. 93, 96). The term *catholic* is an essential

[13] Having said this, we can concentrate our attention on the three *laws* of Christian anxiety (*CA*, 96, 105–6, 114). Balthasar radically distinguishes morbid, psychological ("existentialist") anxiety, which is self-preoccupied, from the anxiety that is the fruit of the Christian's appropriation in the Holy Spirit of Jesus' redemptive anxiety. In so doing he radically distinguishes the disciple's anxiety from the Lord's. There are no other redeemers; no one is on the same level as the one and only Son; the baptized person who shares in the Redeemer's anxiety remains a man and a sinner (*CA*, 104–5). Balthasar thus does justice in a Catholic manner to the Protestant insistence on the absolute uniqueness of the redemptive act and on *sola gratia*.

notion in Balthasar's work. It does not in the first instance denote the beliefs and practices specific to the
"Roman Catholic Church" as opposed to the churches
of the Reformation. Its primary meaning is rather the
abyss of trinitarian Love as revealed and given in the
smallest, most concrete reality of all—the unity of the
infinite and the finite in the flesh and the history of
Jesus of Nazareth. The all-embracing reality of trinitarian love is manifested in the Passion and the Cross,
in the one and only Son, in whom all of us are repre-
sented.

Christian anxiety is *catholic*, because the baptized person who shares in the Redeemer's anxiety no longer
distinguishes his own penance from everyone else's,
no longer judges himself, no longer separates himself
from the sin of all. He knows that a primordial tie binds
him to all men. What he has received as his own talent
and mission is, objectively speaking, for all. This is a
"solidarity" (*CA*, 93) that participates in the specifically christological substitution[14] communicated to the
world in the Church. *Catholic anxiety*, understood in
this sense, is the key to the meaning of the work as a
whole.

Balthasar illustrates the nature of anxiety by means
of *biblical* examples: Lazarus' sisters (Jn 11; cf. *CA*,

---

[14] *CA*, 93. Later soteriology would oppose *solidarity* and *substitution*
(cf. Balthasar himself: *Theo-Drama*, vol. 4: *The Action* [San Francisco:
Ignatius, 1994], 267ff., 290ff.). At the time of writing *The Christian
and Anxiety*, Balthasar successfully maintained a link between them.

91); participation in the fruitful anguish of the Cross (*CA*, 91) which is discussed in the scriptural part of the book; Paul; Daughter Zion; even Job (*CA*, 39).

Balthasar also draws upon *literature* for insights into anxiety, recalling characters who, beyond their natural fearfulness or courage (*CA*, 108–9), have an intimate knowledge of the anxiety and the joy of the Savior, like Bernanos himself in the latter part of his life (*CA*, 108).

Finally, we can examine the way in which the third chapter of the book sheds an *ontological* light on its theological center.

A Debate with Kierkegaard

Balthasar turns to ontology because the Christian is first of all a man. Christian revelation and the life of faith that responds to it are not foreign to man's reality but radicalize and transform it from within by the grace of Christ. If Christian revelation is to take place in history and be received by the human heart, it must incorporate certain anthropological structures prepared beforehand for this supernatural light. A theology of anxiety thus requires philosophical reflection on the condition of possibility of man's anxiety. But how is this philosophical reflection to be conducted?

On this point, Balthasar engages in a very subtle debate with the Kierkegaard of *The Concept of Anxiety*

(1844), to whom he pays tribute and against whom he also raises certain objections. Tribute: Kierkegaard deserves credit for having reflected upon a phenomenon that, while profoundly human, eludes the usual categories of philosophy and for having succeeded in drawing out of it a fundamentally important concept. But Balthasar also pronounces a No: *The Concept of Anxiety* is precisely *not* a theology of anxiety but, despite Kierkegaard's protestations to the contrary, a psychological account influenced by German Idealism. As Balthasar puts it, in Kierkegaard "anxiety remains . . . a matter of the finite mind horrified at its own limitlessness" (*CA*, 32).

As a result, Kierkegaard's analysis, while showing clearly the genesis of man's anxiety in the face of the void that the mind discovers in itself, fails to evidence the mind's openness to divine transcendence. Balthasar agrees that anxiety is immanent in the mind, but he sees the ultimate root of this immanence, not in man's finitude, but in a disorder caused by original sin. Influenced by Lutheran dogmatics, Kierkegaard was unable to see the convergence between philosophical reflection and revelation but remained imprisoned in the abyss of subjectivity. For Balthasar, on the other hand, revelation penetrates and illumines the structure of finitude: anxiety is never merely "natural". It cannot be the object of a purely philosophical concept.

By making explicit the underlying question of original sin (*CA*, 133–38), we can show the similarities and differences between Balthasar's, primarily theological, and Kierkegaard's, strictly philosophical, account of anxiety. For Balthasar, original sin enables us to understand that the void structuring man's acts of knowledge and freedom is not neutral but is a deficiency, indeed, an estrangement from God (*CA*, 140–41). Balthasar's analysis reflects reason's openness to a surplus of meaning (*CA*, 115–17). Kierkegaard, on the other hand, rejecting the state of original justice as a myth (*CA*, 138), precludes the idea that man's relation to God affects the structure of the human spirit.

The Christian and Anxiety: Further Readings in Balthasar

Toward the end of *The Christian and Anxiety*, Balthasar suggests that, strictly speaking, the book would need a fourth part dealing with the Church and anxiety (*CA*, 149): To be a Christian is to be in the Church.

For Balthasar, the clear-cut dialectic between the anxiety of sin and the anxiety of the Cross is also played out within the Church. One may, of course, regard the Church as a handrail that prevents the Christian from making the leap of faith. Nevertheless, the Church can and must be seen, in her essence, as educating man to risk the leap away from all handrails (*CA*, 150). The Church is an environment where even the morbid fear of sinful Christians can, by the Word, prayer, and the sacraments, become the fruitful anxiety of the Cross.

This "paradox of the Church", which Balthasar merely outlines in *The Christian and Anxiety*, brings us indirectly to the context in which the book was written (1951). It required a detour through the Bible, theology, and philosophy to "clarify" (*CA*, 34) what the anxiety of the baptized in the Church and in society can and cannot be. The beautiful concluding pages of *The Christian and Anxiety* are pregnant when read in the context of the painful events leading up to and following the encyclical *Humani Generis* (1950). Hence the observation: "To be a Christian in the Church requires courage" (*CA*, 153). Rather than interpret this remark as a sign of embitterment, however, I think we have to understand it as a token of a great love for the Church. Balthasar often repeated, both before and after Vatican II, that the core of the Church is not the ordained ministry or the Magisterium, but the holiness embodied in the person of Mary. The implicit presence of Mary seems to explain the fundamental distinction between morbid anxiety (the fear of fear) and the fruitful anxiety whose ecclesial and Marian symbol is the Woman of the Apocalypse (*CA*, 77–79; Rev 12:1f.).

For this reason, we would do well to supplement Balthasar's ecclesiological sketch in the last pages of *The Christian and Anxiety* with his reflections on Church and politics in *Bernanos: An Ecclesial Existence*. On a number of points, this later work (1954) further develops the analysis of *The Christian and Anxiety*. Another study that breathes the same atmosphere is Balthasar's 1953 study of Reinhold Schneider.[15] According to Balthasar, Schneider (mentioned on p. 152) had a gift for expressing the tragic character of Christianity: The logic of the Cross cuts through the Church like a fine line dividing holiness and absolute power. Two other books extend the ecclesiological dimension of *The Christian and Anxiety*: *The Office of Peter and the Structure of the Church* and *In the Fullness of the Faith*.[16]

We would misjudge Balthasar's theology if we saw it as a somber enterprise or merely as an exercise in apocalyptic. The passages in which he speaks of the mystery of redemptive substitution and the Christian's participation in it, of joy and the spirit of "childhood" without restless worry, point to the center of his theo-

[15] *Tragedy under Grace: Reinhold Schneider and the Experience of the West* (San Francisco: Ignatius Press, 1997).

[16] In terms of Balthasar's overall work, the christological and soteriological dimension of *The Christian and Anxiety*, with its idea of substitution, has to be seen as part of a continuous theological development founded on the thought of Maximus the Confessor in his battle against Monothelitism (cf. Balthasar's study on Maximus, *Liturgie cosmique* [Paris: Aubier, 1947], in particular 203–5; *Kosmische Liturgie* [Einsiedeln: Johannes Verlag, 1961]; English trans.: *Cosmic Liturgy* [San Francisco: Ignatius Press, 2000]), but also as part of a spiritual line of development beginning with the book *Heart of the World* (*The Christian and Anxiety* is a sort of translation of this lyrical text into the language of biblical, theological, and philosophical analysis. Cf. *Heart of the World* [San Francisco: Ignatius Press, 1979], 107ff., on the "absolute anguish" of Jesus in his substitution for sinners). These two lines converge and reach their high point in *The Threefold Garland* (San Francisco: Ignatius, 1982), and above all in vol. 4 of *Theo-Drama*.

logy. The reader could follow this line of thought from Balthasar's study of Thérèse of Lisieux (1950), through his reflection on "The World of Baptism and Childhood" in *Bernanos: An Ecclesial Existence* and his translation of Marie of the Trinity (1988),[17] up to the posthumously published *Unless You Become Like This Child*.[18]

Karl Barth (1951)—especially the section entitled "The Form and Structure of Catholic Thought"—remains a major source for the theology, in particular the theology of nature and the supernatural, underlying the philosophical discussion in chapter 3 of *The Christian and Anxiety*. Balthasar cites Claudel and Dostoyevsky in order to bring out the social aspect of sin, the substitution of the Redeemer, but also the participation of the justified in the work of redemption in solidarity with all sinners.[19]

Finally, to the extent that this book sets forth a theology of anxiety, which is at once close to, and very different from, existentialism, we could cite the following lines written in 1950:

> [T]he theologian is bound to recognize the approach of existential philosophy as curiously akin to his own. . . .

[17] *Im Schoss des Vaters* ["in the bosom of the Father", an expression dear to Balthasar, which translates John 1:18]. Sister Marie of the Trinity (1903–1980), both through and beyond what she calls her "Job years", knew spiritual childhood and spiritual joy.

[18] English translation by Erasmo Leiva-Merikakis (San Francisco: Ignatius Press, 1991).

[19] *The Theology of Karl Barth* (San Francisco: Ignatius Press, 1992), pt. 3, p. 375, participation as *Mittragen*.

He will do something very different, which is to meet the preoccupations of existential philosophy with *genuine theological statements*, thus working at an existential theology (which is a tautology) not determined by passing influences of fashion. . . . For the business of theology is not to keep one eye on philosophy, but, with its gaze obediently turned toward Jesus Christ, simply and directly to describe how he stands in time and in history as the heart and norm of all that is historical.[20]

Though forty years have passed, *The Christian and Anxiety* shows no signs of aging. We still live in the world of anxiety, and the Christian is always tempted to yield to its morbid fascination.

Existentialism is no longer in fashion as it was after the Second World War. But anxiety remains as does, a fortiori, the mission of the baptized, even with "their anxiety, if God allows it" (*CA*, 156), to be servants of the world's salvation.

To conclude, I would like to say a word about the beauty of Balthasar's theology, which is capable of expressing the splendor, the dramatic breadth, and the incomparable wisdom of the trinitarian love that bears the world and that has been revealed in the anguish and in the glory of Jesus of Nazareth. For in Jesus we know "how much the world matters to [God]" (*CA*, 75).

Yves Tourenne

---

[20] *A Theology of History* (San Francisco: Ignatius Press, 1994), 26–27.

INTRODUCTION

One would not miss the mark if one were to describe
Kierkegaard's lucid and equally profound study of the
"concept of anxiety"[1] as the first and last attempt to
come to terms theologically with his subject. Prior
to this in the history of theology can be found treat-
ments that, at bottom, are no more than what Aristotle
and the Stoics were able to say about this *passio animæ*
[movement of the soul]. Since Thomas Aquinas did not
develop this topic any further, not even the personal
angst of the German Reformer [that is, a salutary fear related to Luther's doctrine of "the bondage of the will"]
was able to have a stimulating effect on systematic
theology, which soon reverted to the schematic formu-
lae of the Scholastic tradition. It took the incipient cosmic anxiety of the modern, secular era, as it began to
smolder beneath the materialism of the eighteenth century and with greater intensity in the postromanticism
of the early nineteenth century (the first squalls presag-
ing today's decline-and-fall psychosis) to convince the
great philosophers to let anxiety have a place in the
heart of ontology and religion. Schelling, Hegel, and
Baader, all three cited by Kierkegaard, were the immediate influences that prompted the Dane to treat this

[1] *Begrebet Angest*, 1844.

theme as a theologian, even if only in an introductory manner (as he puts it, "psychologically" rather than "dogmatically"). He never could bring himself to write a dogmatic tract, and he deliberately posed his questions within a psychological framework—intending, of course, to let the inquiry lead eventually into inevitable dogmatic truth. As a result, anxiety remains for him a matter of the finite mind horrified by its own limitlessness, and God and Christ are rarely mentioned explicitly in this work, which was in fact meant to be an exclusively Christian book. All this, of necessity, helped to determine the book's later destiny: originally a response to philosophical and psychological challenges, it did not free itself sufficiently from them to avoid dissolving again into philosophy, on the one hand, and psychology, on the other, and so its ultimate fate was a twofold secularization. The half-century that intervened between Kierkegaard and Freud and the thirty years between Freud and Heidegger witnessed such a stormy crescendo in the cosmic and existential anxiety of modern man that this and this alone was left as the theme and object for any analysis of anxiety. Though meant to be theological, Kierkegaard's penetrating, tormented analyses were the perfect starting point for psychoanalysis and existentialist philosophy as they portrayed the depths and self-encounters of the finite mind from the perspective of contemporary intellectual attitudes, however dissimilar in intention and method the psychoanalysts and the existentialists may have understood their achievements to be. Although from a theological perspective one may justifiably be critical of both trends, nevertheless facts cannot be denied, and one of the facts is that neither mode of thought was developed out of thin air; rather, both took concrete data about the modern world and the real situation of its subjective and objective spirit as a point of departure and model. Indeed, each in its own way, though perhaps with inadequate means, sought to overcome the anxiety crisis of the modern mind. The absence of a serious theology of anxiety in the face of the rising flood tide, both of anxiety itself and also of philosophical and psychological efforts to interpret and overcome it, became all the more painful when both the phenomenon and the attempts at interpretation rolled over the threshold of the Church and vehemently announced their presence within Christianity itself. It was not merely the ever more frequent charges made by outsiders that Christianity was a religion of anxiety or the efforts of Protestant psychoanalysts both pro and con[2] to determine the degree of truth in Nietzsche's assertion with respect to Christianity in general and the Christian denominations in particular. Even more important was the fact that highly qualified minds at the very heart of the Church were taking up the theme and were developing the description and analysis of

[2] For example, Oskar Pfister, *Das Christentum und die Angst* (Zurich, 1942).

anxiety. As has often happened in recent times, the poets led the way and rushed into the breach left by the theologians: Bloy, Bernanos, and Claudel in France and, in Germany, Gertrud von Le Fort and many others who were interested in Carmelite spirituality. By now if a theologian is to give this topic the treatment that is due to it (as the proverb says, "Better late than never"), he must not only continue along more dogmatic lines the work that Kierkegaard began but also bring to the current controversies inside and outside the Church, which have been driven by partisan animosity, some measure of clarity and calm.

A first step toward clarification might be to realize that an explicitly theological investigation requires that we turn to the sources of revelation and thereby turn away from the uncertainty of the present age and of human frailty. The correct view and explanation of reality, therefore, is based neither on the human mind nor on the soul, which with their anxiety have been the actual object of most recent research; the true standard and guarantee is, rather, the Word of God, which speaks about mind and soul and their anxiety. This is our guarantee that we can gain some distance from the feverish questioning of the modern soul; from its culture, which is supposedly decadent and doomed to destruction; and from its religious anxiety and religion of anxiety, in which, paradoxically enough, the attempts to cure the patient venture into the disease and collapse into one with it, as if it were an unalterable fact to be accepted as a matter of course. The Word of God guarantees an objective distance from those Christian prophets of doom, who apply their misplaced melancholy and radicalism to the task of announcing the immediate and total demise of everything that is of lasting importance in the Church today. They fuse Spengler with the Apocalypse and then imagine that the very fatalism of their vision is their divine authorization to proclaim it. Such prophets are cowards. The Word of God also guarantees us distance from the representatives of the opposite form of cowardice, who ignore the anxiety and bewilderment of the age and, deaf to its lamentation, blithely carry on a serene theology of irrelevance. Freeing ourselves both from that false decadence and from this false escapism, our only alternative is to listen to what the fullness of God's Word says about the very subject that is so harrowing for our age, not merely registering what we hear, but making the effort to understand and appropriate it with respect to the here and now.

Gaining a clear view of divine revelation and giving it a fair hearing will lessen the danger of mistaking a particular, specific form of anxiety, with its specific causes, for the entire phenomenon or even for the most profound element in it, which would restrict the subject from the start. The particular case is the anxiety of modern man in a mechanized world where colossal machinery inexorably swallows up the frail human body and mind only to refashion it into a cog in the machinery—machinery that thus becomes as meaningless as it is all-consuming—the anxiety of man in a civilization that has destroyed all humane sense of proportion and that can no longer keep its own demons at bay. This anxiety underlies almost all modern neuroses—and "modern neurosis" is almost a tautology, inasmuch as there were, strictly speaking, no neuroses in the earlier, humane world (and hence no need for their poisonous antidote, psychotherapy). A theology of anxiety will view this greatly inflated modern anxiety as only *one* expression of the ever-present anxiety in men that revelation considers—since revelation deals with each man and each generation; it will apply to this anxiety the standards valid in heaven and thereby—incidentally yet quite fundamentally—it will also provide standards by which to measure modern anxiety. For it is no secret that the theologian has to explain God's revelation, not as something abstract and self-contained, but in such a way as to make it understandable to the men of his own time, whose understanding is conditioned by their particular needs and cares. The moment a theologian lines up the Scripture passages that deal with anxiety and tries to put them in order, he will discover that they urgently cry out for a rational ordering and then for an interpretation. Indeed, there are contrasting texts that nearly contradict one another, or texts that oppose historical events. For this reason, if one wishes to make sense of them and attribute to them the power to explicate human existence, they should be interpreted within a comprehensive perspective on the meaning of revelation, a framework that can never be unaffected by contemporary thought, that is to say, by that very mankind which is ever being considered and addressed in the present by God's Word. To this extent, supratemporal meaning and contemporary relevance meet and intersect in a theology of anxiety.

Such a theology will have to take as its point of departure the words of Holy Scripture that deal in detail with anxiety, its value and disvalue, its meaning and absurdity. To our knowledge, Christian tradition has never really treated these statements from Scripture thematically but has at best dealt with them indirectly (for example, the distinction between servile fear and filial fear plays a part in the tracts on grace and the sacraments); therefore tradition in this case will have little to contribute. Even in our initial survey of the subject, the statements from Scripture should be arranged so as to indicate at least the outline of an interpretation.

This interpretation is to be developed explicitly in the second part of this book; the multivalence of the phenomenon of anxiety, apparent in the diversity of scriptural references, will be set forth, and necessary distinctions as well as the interrelationships and dynamics among the various levels will be made clear.

The consequent rules for a Christian theology of anxiety and also for the conduct of Christian life are to be formulated as a tangible result.

The third part will proceed to penetrate even deeper and attempt to establish the essence of anxiety. This is where the encounter with the philosophical-theological efforts at interpretation by Kierkegaard and his successors must take place, and it will become evident whether the biblical approach can be more instructive and more profound than the great Danish thinker's "psychological" approach.

I

GOD'S WORD AND ANXIETY

When one surveys even from a distance how often and how openly Sacred Scripture speaks of fear and anxiety, an initial conclusion presents itself: the Word of God is not afraid of fear or anxiety. God's Word enters into this topic with the same mastery that it brings to everything that is characteristically human (and we know humanity only in its fallen state and in the redemption that is under way). For the Word of God, anxiety is not something to be ashamed of, any more than suffering and death are. After all, one function of God's Word is "discerning the thoughts and intentions of the heart . . . before him no creature is hidden, but all are open and laid bare to [his] eyes" (Heb 4:12–13). God's Word is not especially concerned with protecting humanity in this world from suffering and death; neither did the Word enter the world simply to remove anxiety or to preserve people from it as, for example, the philosophy and practical wisdom of the Stoics try to do. In the final analysis, the explicit or implicit purpose of every philosophy and practical wisdom and every spiritual variety of humanism is to show humanity a stance and a perspective from which they can come to terms with these three dark powers.

One cannot maintain the contrary, either: that God's Word has taken a special, as it were, curious interest in the anxiety of mankind and of the creature as such, that it has brought anxiety to light or has proposed or even encouraged anxiety. Instead, God's Word accepts anxiety as a fundamental given of human existence so as to revalue it from God's exalted vantage point, just as everything human is clay in the hands of the Creator and Redeemer. What God makes out of anxiety through this re-creation cannot be deduced in any way from anxiety itself or suspected in advance. The salvation of mankind is not less, but rather more spontaneous than its creation and can only be understood as God's own initiative. As viewed by the Word of God, anxiety is, to begin with, something general and neutral, a basic given of human existence as such:

> Much labor was created for every man,
>> and a heavy yoke is upon the sons of Adam,
>> from the day they come forth from their mother's
>>> womb
>> till the day they return to the mother of all.
>> Their perplexities and fear of heart—
>>> their anxious thought is the day of death,
>> from the man who sits on a splendid throne
>>> to the one who is humbled in dust and ashes,
>> from the man who wears purple and a crown
>>> to the one who is clothed in burlap;
>> there is anger and envy and trouble and unrest,
>>> and fear of death, and fury and strife.
>> And when one rests upon his bed,
>>> his sleep at night confuses his mind.

He gets little or no rest,
   and afterward in his sleep, as though he were on
     watch,
he is troubled by the visions of his mind
   like one who has escaped from the battle-front;
at the moment of his rescue he wakes up,
   and wonders that his fear came to nothing
(Sir 40:1-7).

This anxiety is neutral, having the lofty and the lowly, the priest and the layman in its power, exempting no one from the "mother's womb" even to the "mother of all". Cosmic language is not used idly in this passage, which has to do with a general trait characterizing the earthly creature as such. This is a trait that goes so deep that it reveals an unfathomable quality about life, a sort of bottomlessness from which there is no refuge, no evasion, not even in the hiding place of sleep —certainly not in its supposed unconsciousness. The man who flees from the cares of his waking routine into sleep will find sleep spitting him back out into his routine cares with anxiety redoubled because it is now entirely revealed in its groundlessness. Anxiety is the common denominator for the reality of the day and the unreality of the dream, and the fact that they can converge in this way is precisely the reason that anxiety exists. Already the terrible paradox of Old Testament existence unfolds: it is finite, limited by birth and by the return to "the mother of all"; and, within these two boundaries that stave off the darkness, there is the demand that one stand in God's light and rejoice in his day—his temporal, passing day—and in God's everlasting light.

> But he who is joined with all the living has hope, for a living dog is better than a dead lion. For the living know that they will die, but the dead know nothing, and they have no more reward; but the memory of them is lost. Their love and their hate and their envy have already perished, and they have no more for ever any share in all that is done under the sun.
>
> Go, eat your bread with enjoyment, and drink your wine with a merry heart. . . . Enjoy life with the wife whom you love, all the days of your vain life which he has given you under the sun, because that is your portion in life and in your toil at which you toil under the sun. . . .
>
> Light is sweet, and it is pleasant for the eyes to behold the sun.
>
> For if a man lives many years, let him rejoice in them all; but let him remember that the days of darkness will be many. All that comes is vanity (Eccles 9:4–9; 11:7–8).

Fully aware of the unending darkness that is to come, one is supposed to rejoice, despite one's finitude, in God's unending light, in which one is permitted to stand for a moment. The wheels of one's existence, the things before and after this moment, remain obscure. One does not have to reckon with either of them. One has to orient oneself toward the light that God grants him during his limited days, the light in which the divine gift of love, faith, and hope for the coming Messiah is embodied. For now, no expansion beyond this realm is permitted. It is not that man is unable to see more; rather, it is a question of God's perfect and positive will not to reveal more than this and of man's obedient will to see no more than has been revealed to him. That such an existence is convulsed by anxiety should be no surprise. And meanwhile nothing remains but the gentle admonition to resign oneself to this unavoidable anxiety, not to become frantic in the midst of this anxiety but to accept the fate determined by God:

> Do not fear the sentence of death;
>   remember your former days and the end of life;
> this is the decree from the Lord for all flesh,
>   and how can you reject the good pleasure of the
>   Most High?
> Whether life is for ten or a hundred or a thousand
>   years,
>   there is no inquiry about it in Hades (Sir 41:3-4).

Until now we have spoken about a neutral anxiety that is inherent in existence as such: about the "vanity" of an existence thoroughly negated by the nothingness "before" and "after", a vanity that pertains equally to the good and the wicked, to those who are turned toward God and those who are turned away from God. Now, however, we must complete the thought and note that this neutrality is immediately displaced, down to the very root of existence, by the difference between this turning toward and this turning away. For these two orientations respectively color existential anxiety at its very core with contrasting hues, so much so that the minimum of commonality that permitted us to speak of a universal phenomenon of anxiety, in both the good and the wicked, vanishes and is subsumed into the contrast that divides the anxiety of the wicked from the behavior and the attitude of the good.

A *wicked man's anxiety* is nowhere portrayed with greater theological precision than in the seventeenth chapter of the Book of Wisdom. Just as the entire book is a meditation on the higher or spiritual sense of Israel's covenant history, in which the deeper revealed meaning of the historical facts is illumined by a second, so to speak, reflective revelation; so too in this chapter the Egyptian darkness offers a lucid insight into the primal anxiety of the wicked man wrapped in the darkness that rises out of Sheol, the dark abyss, as the punishment to which God has sentenced him. The process had been described in the Book of Exodus: "Then the Lord said to Moses, 'Stretch out your hand toward heaven that there may be darkness over the land of Egypt, a darkness to be felt.' . . . And there was thick darkness in all the land of Egypt three days; they did not see one another nor did any rise from his place for three days; but all the people of Israel had light where they dwelt" (Ex 10:21–23). Now Wisdom meditates on this event:

Great are thy judgments and hard to describe;
    therefore uninstructed souls have gone astray.
    For when lawless men supposed that they held the
        holy nation in their power,
    they themselves lay as captives of darkness and
        prisoners of long night,
    shut in under their roofs, exiles from eternal
        providence.
    For thinking that in their secret sins they were
        unobserved
    behind a dark curtain of forgetfulness,
    they were scattered, terribly alarmed,
    and appalled by specters.
    For not even the inner chamber that held them
        protected them from fear,
    but terrifying sounds rang out around them,
    and dismal phantoms with gloomy faces appeared.
    And no power of fire was able to give light,
    nor did the brilliant flames of the stars
    avail to illumine that hateful night.
    Nothing was shining through to them
    except a dreadful, self-kindled fire,
    and in terror they deemed the things which they saw
    to be worse than that unseen appearance.
    The delusions of their magic art lay humbled,
    and their boasted wisdom was scornfully rebuked.
    For those who promised to drive off the fears and
        disorders of a sick soul
    were sick themselves with ridiculous fear.
    For even if nothing disturbing frightened them,
    yet, scared by the passing of beasts and the hissing of
        serpents,
    they perished in trembling fear,
    refusing to look even at the air, though it nowhere
        could be avoided.

For wickedness is a cowardly thing, condemned by its
    own testimony;
distressed by conscience, it has always exaggerated the
    difficulties.
For fear is nothing but surrender of the helps that come
    from reason;
and the inner expectation of help, being weak,
prefers ignorance of what causes the torment.
But throughout the night, which was really powerless,
and which beset them from the recesses of powerless
    Hades,
they all slept the same sleep,
and now were driven by monstrous specters,
and now were paralyzed by their souls' surrender,
for sudden and unexpected fear overwhelmed them.
And whoever was there fell down,
and thus was kept shut up in a prison not made of
    iron;
for whether he was a farmer or a shepherd
or a workman who toiled in the wilderness,
he was seized, and endured the inescapable fate;
for with one chain of darkness they all were bound.
Whether there came a whistling wind,
or a melodious sound of birds in wide-spreading branches,
or the rhythm of violently rushing water,
or the harsh crack of rocks hurled down,
or the unseen running of leaping animals,
or the sound of the most savage roaring beasts,
or an echo thrown back from a hollow of the
    mountains,
it paralyzed them with terror.
For the whole world was illumined with brilliant light,
and was engaged in unhindered work,
while over those men alone heavy night was spread,

an image of the darkness that was destined to receive
    them;
but still heavier than darkness were they to themselves.
But for thy holy ones there was very great light
(Wis 17:1–18:1).

This is a portrait of a total anxiety, caused by the outrageous effort to enslave God's people and God's Kingdom on earth. Sentencing the impious to this fear was
in keeping with a special providential plan of the God
who judges (κρίσεις), whereas the immediate cause of
the anxiety was the "night . . . from the recesses of
powerless Hades". This night has an inextricably reciprocal relationship with the anxiety it causes, in that
it simultaneously effects, graphically portrays, and ultimately is caused by that which it is meant to punish, and the self-torment of anxiety is greater than the
darkness itself of Hades. The main effect of darkness
is that it separates, isolates, makes lonely, incarcerates,
shackles, that it ruptures every communication from
one man to another, and this it does effortlessly with
a single chain to which all those isolated are bound.
Now, this effect on sinners is at the same time caused
by the sinners themselves, insofar as they, in sinning,
thought "that in their secret sins they were unobserved
behind a dark curtain of forgetfulness", of lethe (λήθη).
The descent to the river of the netherworld begins already in the subjective isolation of sinning—for sin is
a striving to evade the communication of divine light.
Worse still, in the wish to be forgotten by God lies

one's ultimate self-exclusion from the bright realm of
providence: φυγάδες τῆς αἰωνίου προνοίας means flee-
ing from eternal providence as much as it means exiled
and driven away from it. But the realm that lies outside the illumined circle of providence, the region to
which the sinner tries to flee, is, as the Old Testament
repeatedly testifies, the dark netherworld, with which
God has no dealings. The wicked are always trying to
evade the light of the all-seeing God, so that light itself
becomes for them an object of anxiety:

> By day they shut themselves up;
>   they do not know the light.
> For deep darkness is morning to all of them;
>   for they are friends with the terrors of deep
>   darkness (Job 24:16–17).

> Woe to those who hide deep from the LORD their
>   counsel,
>   whose deeds are in the dark,
>   and who say, "Who sees us? Who knows us?"
> (Is 29:15).

Yet sin against God, the Light, simultaneously shackles the holy people, in which and through which the
communication of divine light in the world is effected:

> For their enemies . . . had kept thy sons imprisoned,
>   through whom the imperishable light of the law was
>   to be given to the world (Wis 18:4).

The loss of the light that binds together, the imprisonment in isolation signifies, moreover, the loss of reality,
incarceration in the world of phantoms and specters.

It is futile to ask whether the apparitions that manifest themselves in the night of anxiety are "subjective" or "objective". Either way, they are empty. They are "images" (ἰδάλματα) and forms without content (φάσματα), dream-figures that mirror in their gloomy and mournful appearance the interior disposition of the one who sees them. These figures acquire their ghostly reality only in the sphere of anxiety, just as the reality of the entire surrounding world, which reaches the senses as sound or light or in some other way, assumes a completely transformed, unreal, and spectral form of, existence. This world is subjective, since its loss of reality stems uniquely from the wicked person with a bad conscience, whereas "the whole world was illumined with brilliant light", and the same objects viewed by light manifest their genuine reality and materiality. Yet the world of darkness is also objective insofar as this loss of reality corresponds to a positive judgment and decree of providence extending the powerless realm, indeed, the realm of impossibility (ἀδύνατον), into the existing regions. The spectral world has as such a kind of counterreality to the degree that it, too, has a "light"—a groundless and therefore meaningless (αὐτομάτη πυρά) light of darkness that becomes an actual "counterlight" to God's light and law. Indeed, on a deeper level it apes the "self-kindling" fire of God in the Burning Bush and in the Pillar of Fire, a fire which, as such, has to be "dreadful" (φόβου πλήρης). This objective-subjective anxiety is essentially groundless, for it consists in abandoning those grounds that can be seen, it is true, only in the light of God, hence, in relinquishing that interior precondition of the mind that enables man to see and interpret the ground and goal of existence [*des Seienden*]. This precondition is portrayed both as the help of rational deliberation (ἀπὸ λογισμοῦ βοηθήματα) and as hope or confidence or courage (προσδοκία), which is simultaneously the knowledge of being dependent on help and a decision of the will to turn to this help. Hard on the heels of the abandonment of reason, the faculty that bravely looks above and beyond itself for help, follow ignorance of reality and cowardice in the face of it, which cause the irrational to be both "driven" about and "paralyzed". Both conditions, though, depend on wickedness, which is designated as the source of the entire inversion and which reveals its inner cowardice not accidentally but necessarily at the point where judgment overtakes it. We have reached the height of absurdity, though, when the very fear-doctors who pretended to free souls from anxiety by the "delusions of their magic art" (indeed, the magicians in Egypt had offered to charm and banish objective anxiety from the souls of Pharaoh and his people when they were afflicted by the first plagues), are now themselves necessarily beset by anxiety and spellbound,[1] together with their science, thus becoming a monument to God's judgment on the wicked.

[1] *Gebannt*, a German word that can mean both "exiled" and "spellbound". The wordplay cannot be reproduced in English. TRANS.

Taken all together, a picture of total anxiety is presented here, which is bracketed off from reality as a
whole and confined within an anxiety cosmos of its
own, which, as opposed to reality, appears meaningless and devoid of being and nevertheless derives from
this its substance and a manner of meaning and of being peculiar to itself alone. It is a cosmos of anxiety
that is constructed entirely from anxiety, in which everything is a function of anxiety—even breathing the
empty air and every phenomenon occupying space and
time. This world, too, has its magnitude, and even an
unforeseeable potential for being "yet-greater", since
behind each anxiety one suspects, indeed anxiously ex-
pects, a new and deeper one. "Fear works in a double
manner: it despairs of the possibility of help yet height-
ens the pain by admitting, besides despair, no reflection on or thought about the basis for the anxiety. It
is nothing but blind fear, which, beyond the present
suffering, imagines an endless variety of others as possible, indeed, as certain" (Loch and Reischl comment-
ing on the passage from Wisdom). In the final analysis, though, the portrayal of the total anxiety of the
wicked in the Book of Wisdom takes an indeterminate, middle position: on the one hand, it is "an image of the darkness that was destined to receive them",
in other words, a picture of the definitive nothingness
of the darkness that follows death; yet, on the other
hand, it is, within the context of the entire book, only
an image, since God punishes even his enemies with

a certain leniency, with a justice that is tempered by
patience and kindness:

> For thou lovest all things that exist,
>> and hast loathing for none of the things which thou
>> hast made,
>> for thou wouldst not have made anything if thou hadst
>> hated it. . . .
> Thou sparest all things, for they are thine, O Lord
>> who lovest the living (Wis 11:24, 26).

And this applies to those impious ones:

> For thy all-powerful hand,
>> which created the world out of formless matter,
>> did not lack the means to send upon them a multitude
>> of bears, or bold lions,
>> or newly created unknown beasts full of rage,
>> or such as breathe out fiery breath,
>> or belch forth a thick pall of smoke,
>> or flash terrible sparks from their eyes;
>> not only could their damage exterminate men,
>> but the mere sight of them could kill by fright
>> (Wis 11:17-19).

It is very important in the overall theology of anxiety
in Scripture that God did not create such animals. Instead he is content with plagues of vermin and locusts,
whose fluttering and chirping alone nearly kills those
who cower anxiously in the darkness. For the present
it is enough that the wicked are afraid of Nothing, of
nothing real: "The wicked flee when no one pursues"

(Prov 28:1). "They were in great fear where no fear was" (Ps 53:6, Confraternity Version).

For *the good*, a mighty and categorical No stands in opposition to this anxiety of the wicked.

They are absolutely forbidden to know this fear. They should not, they need not enter into it. Already the Old Covenant resounds with the cry: "Fear not!" (Is 41:10), "Fear not, for I have redeemed you" (Is 43:1). Indeed, complete, constant anxiety has as its extreme antithesis the constant absence of anxiety in the good: "So also a fearful heart in the imagination of a fool shall not resist against the violence of fear. As a fearful heart in the thought of a fool at all times will not fear, so neither shall he that continueth always in the commandments of God" (Sir 22:22–23 Douay-Rheims). "Do not fear what they fear, nor be in dread" (Is 8:12). It is clear that this is no moral prohibition, but rather one determined by the supernatural covenant and by the faith that is based upon it. Because the God of the covenant is with him, the believer is not allowed to know fear. That would be the same as unbelief:

> With the Lord on my side I do not fear.
>   What can man do to me? (Ps 118:6; cf. Ps 56:4).

> Therefore we will not fear though the earth should
>   change,
>   though the mountains shake in the heart of the sea;

> though its waters roar and foam,
>   though the mountains tremble with its tumult
> (Ps 46:2–3 [46:3–4]).

> I am not afraid of ten thousands of people
>   who have set themselves against me round about
> (Ps 3:6 [3:7]).

> Even though I walk through the valley of the shadow
>   of death,
>   I fear no evil;
> for thou art with me (Ps 23:4).

> The LORD is my light and my salvation;
>   whom shall I fear?
> The LORD is the stronghold of my life;
>   of whom shall I be afraid?
> When evildoers assail me,
>   uttering slanders against me,
> my adversaries and foes,
>   they shall stumble and fall (Ps 27:1–2).

Even the night holds no terror for the good:

> If you sit down, you will not be afraid;
>   when you lie down, your sleep will be sweet.
> Do not be afraid of sudden panic,
>   or of the ruin of the wicked (Prov 3:24–25).

> He who listens to me will dwell secure
>   and will be at ease, without dread of evil
> (Prov 1:33).

Freedom from anxiety is intimately connected with dwelling in the land of the promise and of grace (Deut

12:10; 1 Kings 5:4; Ezek 34:27), and this bounded-
ness of the earthly region chosen by God and given to
his people characterizes, in turn, the things that per-
tain to the Old Testament. Believing and the grace of
dwelling here stand and fall together. As long as the
people believes, the land is granted to it, as well as
victory in every battle for the land. The strict command to believe and the strict prohibition of anxiety
are completely united, so much so that anyone who is
anxious must be dismissed from the army before the
battle and sent home:

> And when you draw near to the battle, the priest shall
> come forward and speak to the people, and shall say
> to them: "Hear, O Israel, you draw near this day to
> battle against your enemies: let not your heart faint; do
> not fear, or tremble, or be in dread of them; for the
> LORD your God is he that goes with you, to fight for
> you against your enemies, to give you the victory". . . .
> "What man is there that is fearful and fainthearted? Let
> him go back to his house, lest the heart of his fellows
> melt as his heart" (Deut 20:2–4, 8).

Yet this region of freedom from anxiety is established by a God who is himself surrounded by fear
and trembling, whether we consider his essence, his
outreach to man in the mystery of election, or finally
the divine destiny into which he guides his chosen one.
Open the Old Testament to whatever page you want:
it will always mention the *good man's anxiety* about
his relationship with God. At the most profound level

this is related to the finitude of the region of light in which the righteous man stands. To put it more pointedly: it is dependent on the structure of symbol and of promise characterizing the entire covenant, which as such is not yet redemption, not yet a final remission of sin, but is a humanly inconceivable step toward it. The God who has not yet become man remains the Wholly Other, but he does not abide in some vague and remote *mysterium tremendum* (with which God has nonsensically been confused or equated). He is, rather, a God who speaks, who approaches man and casts him down, who demands complete loyalty of him and, as a sign of this loyalty, requires the observance of all his commands. For these reasons he is a God who in a terrifying, overwhelming manner becomes concrete for man—a God who, to put it another way, necessarily spreads anxiety. Yahweh in his divine majesty comes closer to man in the Old Covenant than in the New. He assails man unsparingly and snatches man to himself with no preliminary courtship (this is done later at the Incarnation). He manifests himself in his Godhead so nakedly (whereas the Incarnation will be like a protective covering) that man scarcely understands the love that is revealed in this impetuous ardor (or rather, that is concealed because it is so dazzling). Confused, man lowers his eyes and draws back, conscious of his sinful unworthiness. And so it seems as if God had wanted too much, as if he had been compelled by the anxious trembling of the human heart, which he intended to possess completely, to conceal himself more deeply: in the human form itself. And yet this concealment will be a more profound unveiling, which can be understood as an unveiling only if one has recognized and experienced the flaming nakedness of the Old Covenant.

Here the God who delivers himself up is "a devouring fire, a jealous God" (Deut 4:24) to the creature, so much so that to see him and to live are incompatible things—hence, Isaiah considers himself lost because he has seen the King with his own eyes (Is 6:5), and Daniel, stunned, falls on his face in a deep sleep before him (Dan 10:9). After issuing the command to fear none of the things that make the wicked anxious, God has to add: "The LORD of hosts . . . let him be your fear, and let him be your dread" (Is 8:13). If he snatches up a man or a people to himself, it is in a lightning-stroke of divine election, drawing the elect into the smoke and darkness of his divinity. So it was back in the covenant with Abraham, when, "as the sun was going down, a deep sleep fell on Abram; and lo, a dread and great darkness fell upon him", and "when the sun had gone down and it was dark, behold, a smoking fire pot and a flaming torch" passed through the divided altar as a sign that God himself had sworn this oath of covenant (Gen 15:12, 17–18). So it was again when God stretched forth his hand to his people in Egypt: "Has any god ever attempted to go and take a nation for himself from the midst of another

nation, by trials, by signs, by wonders, and by war, by
a mighty hand and an outstretched arm, and by great
terrors, according to all that the LORD your God did
for you in Egypt" (Deut 4:34). All of this was sealed
in the lightning, the smoke, and the darkness at Sinai
when the covenant was established with the people
in the wilderness. Through such a night of election
man is led into the light of the promise and of the
Promised One. But how can man withstand such a
partner? The devouring purity in which he is invited
to live only uncovers more and more profoundly his
failure, his apostasy, his stubborn inability and unwill-
ingness. As a result, the actual story of God's dealings
with his people is played out, not on the calm plain
of freedom from anxiety, as was to be expected, but
rather at its edges: where God, threatening with all the
means afforded by anxiety, compels man into freedom
from anxiety; where man wavers in fear, wondering
whether God will yet again acknowledge and keep in
force the covenant that has been broken a thousand
times; where the people anxiously fight their way out
of anxiety and into freedom from anxiety.

Thus, on the one hand, is God's challenge to make
an absolute decision for him, whereby the promise of
freedom from anxiety is found in a resolute decision.
On the other hand, though, behind the necessity of de-
ciding, all the sanctions of anxiety are threatening, to
such an extent that the covenant promised as something
final is made out to be conditional, something that,

under certain circumstances, must be declared anew—precisely because its finality is so serious. There is the command to advance into freedom from anxiety but also the dire warning not to turn back because that would entail all manner of anxiety:

> But if you will not obey the voice of the LORD your God or be careful to do all his commandments and his statutes which I command you this day, . . . the LORD will send upon you curses, confusion, and frustration, in all that you undertake to do. . . . The LORD will smite you with madness and blindness and confusion of mind; and you shall grope at noonday, as the blind grope in darkness. . . . And he will bring upon you again all the diseases of Egypt, which you were afraid of; and they shall cleave to you. . . . And the LORD will scatter you among all peoples. . . . And . . . you shall find no ease, and there shall be no rest for the sole of your foot; but the LORD will give you there a trembling heart, and failing eyes, and a languishing soul; your life shall hang in doubt before you; night and day you shall be in dread, and have no assurance of your life. . . . And the LORD will bring you back in ships to Egypt, a journey which I promised that you should never make again (Deut 28:15, 20, 28–29, 60, 64–66, 68).

Indeed, the Egyptian plagues become altogether concrete in the threat:

> And I will devastate the land, . . . and I will unsheathe the sword after you. . . . And as for those of you that are left, I will send faintness into their hearts in the lands of

their enemies; the sound of a driven leaf shall put them
to flight, and they shall flee as one flees from the sword,
and they shall fall when none pursues (Lev 26:32–33,
36).

This thousandfold threat, which re-echoes through
the entire law and all of the prophets, is so terrifying
that the person who runs into some earthly distress
never knows whether this threat might not be starting
to materialize. The command to be fearless stands before him, to be sure, but as he reaches for it, waves of
anxiety engulf him, and his relationship to God consists in the struggle to catch hold of the plank in time.

This battle which anxiety wages for fearlessness in
the face of God has various stages and levels, even in
the Old Testament relationship with God. Initially it is
the relatively external situation, the subject of so many
psalms, in which the man who is true to the covenant
is overwhelmed by the superior power of God's enemies. In this case, therefore, it is anxiety's simple plea
to God:

> Give ear to my prayer, O God;
>   and hide not thyself from my supplication!
> Attend to me, and answer me;
>   I am overcome by my trouble.
> I am distraught by the noise of the enemy,
>   because of the oppression of the wicked. . . .
> My heart is in anguish within me,
>   the terrors of death have fallen upon me.
> Fear and trembling come upon me,
>   and horror overwhelms me.

And I say, "O that I had wings like a dove!
  I would fly away and be at rest" (Ps 55:1–6).

This is anxiety of an entirely human sort, which opens up to God and expresses itself, in which is mixed at the same time anxiety for God's reign and justice, thereby becoming a substitute anxiety for God. As such it is entitled to demand help that much more urgently. And so, to the anxiety of God's servant, who cries out to God in the most profound anxiety "from the torrents of perdition" and the "cords of Sheol", salvation by God can be portrayed as a theophany of anxiety in which God draws near with all the regalia of horror —in the presence of which "the channels of the sea [are] seen and the foundations of the world [are] laid bare"—in order to save the supplicant:

He reached from on high, he took me,
  he drew me out of many waters.
He delivered me from my strong enemy
  (Ps 18:16–17; cf. 2 Sam 22:1–20).

But from here it is only a small step to the anxiety experienced by the "righteous" man who, again and again failing, falling away, or lulling himself in false security, is led by God to the utmost brink of anxiety, so that he might pray himself back, with greater awareness and gratitude, into the midst of hope. The man in Psalm 107 is led into a fourfold temptation —thirst in the wilderness, imprisonment in darkness and the shadow of death, a sickness unto death with loathing and disgust for every sort of food, a storm at sea that tosses the ship to the heights and into the depths. What matters to the Psalmist is not the description of the trials but their objective: to coax from the endangered person an anxious cry to God: "Then they cried to the LORD in their trouble, and he delivered them from their distress." Whether the prisoners "rebelled against the words of God, and spurned the counsel of the Most High", whether the sick "because of their iniquities suffered affliction", or whether the wanderers in the wilderness simply lost their way, apart from any question of guilt, or whether the seafarers were merely supposed to have an opportunity to see the greatness of God's marvelous works on the ocean—the reason for the trial has become almost irrelevant. Both explanations, the human guilt that deserves tribulation and God's will to reveal his glory in the tribulation, stand side by side without tension, complementing each other. Indeed, it all culminates in the storm at sea which God himself willed and stirred up:

> For he commanded, and raised the stormy wind,
>   which lifted up the waves of the sea.
> They mounted up to heaven, they went down to the
>   depths;
>   their courage melted away in their evil plight;
> they reeled and staggered like drunken men,
>   and were at their wits' end.
> Then they cried to the LORD in their trouble,
>   and he delivered them from their distress;

he made the storm be still,
   and the waves of the sea were hushed
   (Ps 107:25–29).

It is essential that, for human beings, both reasons for the tribulation—their own guilt, which leads them to the brink of being abandoned, and their exposure to God's storm-waves—are indistinguishable to those in the midst of tribulation and anxiety. What matters and what God wants to hear is the anxious cry sent up to him, which, the moment it is sounded, even from the farthest coast, also reaches the center of God's heart. It is in "hanging by a thread"—provided the thread is God—that the covenant relationship is tested anew and restored.

Thus the darkness of the threatened curse, which was shown to the people as lying *behind* them but which was held out as a real possibility in the case of apostasy, can ultimately, in time of trial, come to lie *in front* of the man being tested (regardless of whether he is righteous or a sinner who needs to be brought back). And this is a darkness that, because it is God's, does without the "indulgences" granted by providence in Egypt. The "vermin" and the "locusts" are replaced by full-grown "beasts" with open jaws snapping: the "bulls", the "strong bulls", the "ravening and roaring lions" with mouths "open wide", the pack of "dogs", and the "horns of the wild oxen" of Psalm 22 and finally by the menagerie of monsters God deploys against Job (Job 40–41), which appear like precursors to the beasts of the Apocalypse. The enemies advance against Job:

> He has torn me in his wrath, and hated me;
>   he has gnashed his teeth at me (16:9).

Job complains to God:

> thou dost scare me with dreams and terrify me with visions,
> so that I would [rather] choose strangling (7:14–15).

"Amid thoughts from visions of the night" he hears a whispered word from God that causes "dread" to come over him and "trembling" to make all his bones shake (Job 4:12–15). Job is the man who is terrified at the presence of God (23:15). In Job's anxiety we see the Old Testament anxiety of the righteous man consummated and capsized. To the subjective inability to distinguish, in a state of anxiety, between one's own guilt and God's testing is joined an objective dialectic (which will later be Kafka's starting point): on the one hand, between Job's friends and accusers, who bring out the inevitability of guilt, and the sufferer, who protests his innocence; on the other hand, within Job himself, between God's own declaration of Job's guilt, which is incomprehensible to him in his anxiety, and Job's consciousness of his innocence:

> If it is a matter of justice, who can summon him?
> Though I am innocent, my own mouth would
>   condemn me;

> though I am blameless, he would prove me
>   perverse.
> I am blameless! . . .
> I shall be condemned;
>   why then do I labor in vain?
> If I wash myself with snow,
>   and cleanse my hands with lye,
> yet thou wilt plunge me into a pit,
>   and my own clothes will abhor me
> (Job 9:19–21, 29–31).

Job stands in the nakedness of fear before God. Every earthly covering is ripped away from him at the start, all his worldly supports are removed, so that later, when the real tribulation begins, nothing remains but for him to be the abandoned one, the man delivered over to anxiety. Here it becomes evident that man cannot live in such immediacy; he will be burned up by the sheer superiority of God's power. No arrangement, no agreement, no dialogue is possible where the naked Absolute and the naked Contingent collide. Job cries out, not for his children, his property, his wife, his friends, but for a mediator:

> Would that there were an umpire [adjudicator]
>   between us,
>   who might lay his hand upon us both.
> Let him take his [God's] rod away from me,
>   and let not dread of him terrify me (9:33–34).

He cries out for justice with God, which can come to him only from God; he appeals from God to God (16:19–20): from a hidden, absent, and incomprehen-

sible God to One who would turn toward man in a
human way (23:1–7); from a God who for him has
"changed into a Satan" and whom one can no longer
call upon since he has become an unmitigated No, to
a God who, beyond all dialectic of anxiety, would simply say Yes to man.

Here the night-zone that surrounded the cone of
light marked out by Old Testament finitude has completely inundated and submerged the narrow strip of
secure land. The already dialectical situation of decid-
ing (for God and for non-anxiety, but under the threat
of anxiety) is once again surpassed by a situation that
God alone has established and for which only he can
be responsible. God's promise of freedom from anxiety is overtaken by God himself, and the earlier dialectic (so stubbornly defended by Job's "friends") is
brushed aside (42:7–9), because the finitude of the
Old Covenant is now manifested in itself, that is, it
is shown to have reached its end. At the very moment when anxiety floods the center (and not just the
periphery) of the region that had been spared, when
the Egyptian darkness and the soul's "waters of chaos"
are unleashed from the prisons of Hades and the su-
perterrestrial dungeons and engulf the "holy land",
the countermovement has necessarily, though invisibly,
taken place: the former finite borderline against chaos
has been removed by God, and the New Covenant is
within view.

Hence, in a preliminary consideration, one can speak

of two kinds of anxiety in the Old Covenant: an anxiety of the wicked and an anxiety of the good. They are diametrically opposed to each other: the anxiety of wicked men is futile and, viewed from the light that surrounds the righteous, it is ludicrous; the anxiety of good men, since it is permitted and willed by God, is a right and earnest fear. The anxiety of the wicked is an anticipation of the darkness of Hades, and the light within it is deceptive, for this anxiety is a lasting condition, while the anxiety of good men is a process, a passage, an episode between light and light. The anxiety of the wicked is both effect and cause of their turning away from God; it encloses and incarcerates; it is the sign of God's wrath set up over them—whereas the anxiety of the good has as its meaning and purpose to open them up to God in their cry for mercy; it is the banner of God's grace unfurled over them. Yet the distinction, however correct it may be, is still only provisional: in the first place, because in the anxiety of the wicked also a "gracious providence" governs; then again and more importantly, because even the righteous man falls and because, in an extravagant and incomprehensible turn of events, he can be led into the anxiety reserved for the wicked or, indeed, an anxiety from which the wicked are preserved.

One cannot portray Old Testament existence as a sort of "balance" between anxiety and hope, anxiety and assurance of salvation; that would be to oversimplify its unprecedented drama. The prohibition of anxiety and the command to hope—to entrust and submit oneself to the God of the covenant—are much rather like a course that is to be held unwaveringly. Neither falling back into sin (and thus into the anxiety that lies behind man) nor the experience of being led into tribulation (and thus into a not explicitly announced, hence unexpected and incomprehensible, anxiety that lies before man and which God has created and is responsible for) may throw him off this course. Everything depends on not going astray. Anxiety thereby has become a multivalent, malleable phenomenon, which, in the hand of God, is capable of serving the most varied purposes. The New Testament will be the equal of the Old in this multivalence, even though the overall phenomenon of anxiety undergoes at this stage a complete revaluation and reorganization.

In the *New Covenant* it appears at first glance that the Old is not abrogated; it is taken over in order to be completed. And this completion does not take place without a deepening of anxiety. In the first place, the general fear of meeting God in the Judgment—a fear of mankind as a whole that was already known in the Old Covenant—appears again. Even back in the Old Covenant, the "day of the Lord" was the "great and very terrible" day of days (Joel 2:11). "But who can endure the day of his coming, and who can stand when he appears? For he is like a refiner's fire and like fullers' soap" (Mal 3:2). This is

a day of distress and anguish,
a day of ruin and devastation,
a day of darkness and gloom (Zeph 1:15).

"Wail, for the day of the LORD is near" (Is 13:6). It is the day about which now Christ too proclaims: "There will be signs in sun and moon and stars, and upon the earth distress of nations in perplexity at the roaring of the sea and the waves, men fainting with fear and with foreboding of what is coming on the world; for the powers of the heavens will be shaken" (Lk 21:25–26). This is the day on which people of every rank will crawl away and call out to the mountains and rocks: "Fall on us and hide us from the face of him who is seated on the throne, and from the wrath of the Lamb; for the great day of their wrath has come, and who can stand before it?" (Rev 6:16–17). Yet the opposite happens: "The sky vanished like a scroll that is rolled up, and every mountain and island was removed from its place" (6:14); "earth and sky fled away, and no place was found for them" (20:11)—so that man in complete nakedness may meet his judge.

The anxiety of the wicked man appears in the eschatological visions of the New Covenant intensified beyond all that went before. For the darkness that had ascended from the Hades or Sheol of the Old Testament now darkens once again into the gloomy realm of the final abyss of hell, which only begins to yawn in view of the fullness of grace and salvation. "He opened the shaft of the bottomless pit, and from the shaft rose

smoke like the smoke of a great furnace, and the sun
and the air were darkened with the smoke from the
shaft'' (Rev 9:2). And this time it is no longer harmless
locusts that frighten the fearful during the night; rather,
the very gloom and smoke condense into locusts, as if
darkness itself had become an animal and an onslaught.
And the locusts in turn consolidate into monsters that
in every single attribute are nothing other than the ag-
glomeration of all that is ghastly and horrifying:

> Then from the smoke came locusts on the earth, and
> they were given power like the power of scorpions of
> the earth. . . . In appearance the locusts were like horses
> arrayed for battle; on their heads were what looked like
> crowns of gold; their faces were like human faces, their
> hair like women's hair, and their teeth like lions' teeth;
> they had scales like iron breastplates, and the noise of
> their wings was like the noise of many chariots with
> horses rushing into battle. . . . The number of the troops
> of cavalry was twice ten thousand times ten thousand; I
> heard their number. And this was how I saw the horses
> in my vision: the riders wore breastplates the color of
> fire and of sapphire and of sulphur, and the heads of the
> horses were like lions' heads, and fire and smoke and
> sulphur issued from their mouths. . . . The power of the
> horses is in their mouths and in their tails; their tails are
> like serpents, with heads, and by means of them they
> wound (Rev 9:3, 7–9, 16–17, 19).

The vision of anxiety found in the Book of Wisdom
has been heightened to an unimaginable degree. Each
superlative surpasses itself again: the smoke is an an-

imal, the locust is a scorpion, the scorpion bears the marks of every predatory beast, the attack becomes an overwhelming battle raging on all sides, the number of the attackers is multiplied fantastically, and the entire scene dissolves into a surging sea of flames, each one of which nevertheless strikes home, in precisely the manner least expected: for they conceal their ultimate malice in their tails. If one adds to this all the remaining terrors of the Apocalypse, its numbers, trumpets, and riders, at the end of divine revelation stands a vision of anxiety that qualitatively encompasses and exceeds everything in the Old Testament. Nonetheless everything stands—and this is what is New—within a bracket: the bracket of the vision, and this gives it a special form of divine, absolute truth, which then also illuminates retroactively the form of truth expressed as a threat in Old Testament law and prophecy.

The *anxiety of the good* also is brought to the height of intensity in the final Covenant—at the point where the incarnate God sends his chosen disciples out onto the lake alone at dusk:

> The boat by this time was many furlongs distant from the land, beaten by the waves; for the wind was against them. And in the fourth watch of the night he came to them, walking on the sea. But when the disciples saw him walking on the sea, they were terrified, saying, "It is a ghost!" And they cried out for fear. But immediately he spoke to them, saying, "Take heart, it is I; have no fear" (Mt 14:24–27).

Whereas in Psalm 107 God himself stirred up the storm at sea and willed the anxiety of the mariners, and whereas in the Book of Wisdom the world had become a ghostly apparition to the anxious, here we find both precedents surpassed in that God himself appears ghostlike to them in the situation of anxiety he has ordered. The selfsame God who has revealed himself, who has overcome the distance between them and himself in order to shut the abyss of anxiety—he it is who acts like a ghost, turns into a phantom. In the first instance of a storm at sea, when he was among them sleeping in the boat and they anxiously awoke him, he still scolded them: "Why are you afraid? Have you no faith?" (Mk 4:40). At this, "they were filled with awe" of him whom the wind and sea obey. In the second instance he does not scold them any more: he himself sent them into the night and did nothing to dispel what was fearful and spectral in their hearts or in his appearance: this is how he wanted to be apprehended this time. It is revelation in anxiety, a continuation of Job's dark night, in which God's face is so altered for the fearful one that he no longer recognizes it. Within the brackets of this extreme situation are contained all the anxieties of the New Covenant: the anxieties of all those to whom God comes with immediacy and who draw back trembling, like Zechariah (Lk 1:12); Mary (Lk 1:29); Joseph (Mt 1:20); Peter (Lk 5:8–9); the disciples on Mount Tabor (Mt 17:6); all the disciples at so many terrifying words of the Lord (Mk 10:25); those who flee during his Passion (Mk 14:50); the women at the tomb who "fled . . . for trembling and astonishment had come upon them; and they said nothing to any one, for they were afraid" (Lk 24:22; Mk 16:8); the apostles who see the Risen One and "were startled and frightened, and supposed that they saw a spirit" (Lk 24:37); Paul, who stands before Christ's appearance "trembling and astonished" (Acts 9:6, Vulgate and Douay versions); the seer of Patmos, who collapses as if dead before the Son of Man (Rev 1:17).

Yet all these anxieties surrounding the Incarnate One like a nimbus are subsumed and rendered unimportant by the *anxiety of the Redeemer* himself, which signifies the difference between the anxiety of the Old and that of the New Covenant, a difference that is unique yet revalues everything. The Old Covenant had advanced as far as the anguish of Job: the intrusion of darkness into the finite realm of faith's light. This transgression of the old order could be ventured only as an anticipation of the Cross, of God's own anguish. God could not become man in any other way than by coming to know human fear and by taking it upon himself:

> Since . . . the children [of God] share in flesh and blood, he himself likewise partook of the same nature, that through death he might destroy him who has the power of death, that is, the devil, and deliver all those who through fear of death were subject to life-

long bondage. . . . Therefore he had to be made like his
brethren in every respect. . . . For because he himself
has suffered and been tempted, he is able to help those
who are tempted (Heb 2:14–18).

"In every respect [he] has been tempted as we are,
yet without sinning" (Heb 4:15). "In the days of his
flesh, Jesus offered up prayers and supplications, with
loud cries and tears, to him who was able to save him
from death, and he was heard for his godly fear" (Heb
5:7)—heard, not in that anxiety was spared him, but
in that it was granted and entrusted to him to the
utmost degree. It rolls toward him in waves: at the
grave of Lazarus it is an initial "shudder" as he brushes
against the world of the dead, against the soon-to-be-
unsealed abyss of smoke and darkness (Jn 11:33–38).
Shortly thereafter, in the temple, it is a new "shudder"
at what is now certain because sealed by the Father's
voice: the inevitability of his hour (Jn 12:27-28). On
the Mount of Olives it is a final, precipitous plunge
into the abyss of anxiety that immediately breaks over
him: vicariously, for every sinner and every sin, he
suffers the anxiety of facing the God of absolute righteousness. All that the Old and New Covenants know
of anxiety is here gathered together and infinitely surpassed, because the person who in this human nature
is frightened is the infinite God himself. It is, first of
all, the suffering of the infinitely Pure One, the infinitely Righteous One (who is also God) when con-

fronted with all that God abhors and that can reveal its full hideousness only to the Pure One (who is also God). It is, furthermore, the vicarious suffering of this Pure One for all the impure, that is, experiencing that anxiety which every sinner by right would have to go through before the judgment seat of God and in being rejected by him. It is, finally and most profoundly, the anguish that God (in human form) suffers on account of his world, which is in danger of being lost to him—which, indeed, at that moment *is* an utterly lost world. So as to be able to suffer this anxiety and therein to demonstrate humanly how much the world matters to him in his divinity and how concerned he is for the world's sake: for this purpose he became man. It is an anguish he wanted to have without any consolation or relief, since from it was to come every consolation and relief for the world. Therefore it is, in the proper and strict sense of the word, the absolute anxiety, which undergirds and surpasses every other anxiety and thus becomes the standard and tribunal for all. This anxiety is drained to the dregs upon the Cross in the actual abandonment of the Son by the Father. Since the subject who endures this abandonment in his human nature is divine, it is an absolute forsakenness and therefore the absolute measure of the abyss (ἄβυσσος) and of every other abysmal experience. Only the Son knows exhaustively what it means to be forsaken by the Father, for he alone knows who the Father is and what the Father's intimacy and love are.

Every Old Testament experience of anxiety possessed
an exterior, which set a limit to it. Thus during the
Egyptian darkness the holy people found themselves in
the midst of light, and from within this light of the
law and of wisdom, the experience of darkness could
be observed and its intrinsic futility pondered. The experience of anxiety in the Psalms likewise had as its
point of departure faith and, therefore, light. Even Job's
dark night was illuminated by a wisdom, albeit an inaccessible, hidden, "rumored" one, which God alone
knows (Job 28). For the "Book of Job", too, belongs
to the "wisdom books", and the horrible darkening
in the middle of it is bracketed between the light at
the beginning and the end. On the Cross there is no
more "book of wisdom", for the Light of the world
itself has been obscured, "the hour of darkness" has
overpowered it, the wisdom of God as a whole has
become "folly" so as to "destroy the wisdom of the
wise" (1 Cor 1:21, 19). At the moment of this darkening there is no exterior, for all "observation" and all
"meditation" on the event are drawn in and submerged
in the sheer event. This event is now the absolute toward which all the wisdom of creation and of God's
grace-filled ways was conceived and directed and from
which wisdom will be permitted to exist once more
—a new wisdom because it will have shared in the
burial and Resurrection. Into this darkness all things
are darkened as well: "Now from the sixth hour there
was darkness over all the land until the ninth hour. And

about the ninth hour Jesus cried with a loud voice: 'Eli, Eli, lama sabachthani?' that is, 'My God, my God, why hast thou forsaken me?' . . . And the earth shook, and the rocks were split; the tombs also were opened" (Mt 27:45–46, 51–52). The signs of the Judgment come to pass in nature, but also the signs of the bursting of the gates of hell: any place from which the smoke of the abyss can rise up through the cloven earth is a place to which the light of salvation, after its setting, is able to penetrate.

Thus the event interprets itself with the image of the anguished labor pains before birth. In the Old Covenant this was the image for the anxiety of Judgment Day:

> They will be in anguish like a woman in travail.
> They will look aghast at one another;
>   their faces will be aflame (Is 13:8).

> Like a woman with child,
>   who writhes and cries out in her pangs,
>   when she is near her time,
> so were we because of thee, O LORD;
>   we were with child, we writhed,
>   we have as it were brought forth wind
> (Is 26:17–18).

And then it was the image for every futile fear:

> For I heard a cry as of a woman in travail,
>   anguish as of one bringing forth her first child,
> the cry of the daughter of Zion, gasping for breath
> (Jer 4:31).

Damascus has become feeble, she turned to flee,
    and panic seized her;
anguish and sorrows have taken hold of her,
    as of a woman in travail (Jer 49:24).

The king of Babylon heard the report of them,
    and his hands fell helpless;
anguish seized him,
    pain as of a woman in travail (Jer 50:43).

O inhabitant of Lebanon,
. . . how you will groan when pangs come upon you,
    pain as of a woman in travail (Jer 22:23).

Now why do you cry aloud?
    Is there no king in you?
Has your counselor perished,
    that pangs have seized you like a woman in travail?
Writhe and groan, O daughter of Zion,
    like a woman in travail (Micah 4:9–10).

The anguish of Eve and of her curse (Gen 3:16) resounds from the Old Testament image, in which
fecundity seems to have no part. Anxiety as contraction, constriction, cramping: that is all that the image of birth in the Old Covenant yields. If any fruit
is mentioned it is merely "wind". Only in the New
Covenant, in the anguished bringing-forth upon the
Cross, is the image fulfilled with the complete meaning, which surpasses the childbearing of Eve: "When
a woman is in travail she has sorrow, because her hour
has come; but when she is delivered of the child, she
no longer remembers the anguish, for joy that a child
is born into the world" (Jn 16:21).

From the perspective of the anguished bringing-forth of the new aeon upon the Cross, all subsequent anxiety is seen now to be revalued. Now it is possible for anxiety to participate in the fruitful anguish of the Cross. In this sense Paul's "afflictions, hardships, calamities" (2 Cor 6:4) become insignia of his apostolate and, in Christ, Paul becomes the birthgiver of the community (1 Cor 4:15); mindful of the Cross, he stayed with the community "in weakness and in much fear and trembling" (1 Cor 2:3). "Who is weak, and I am not weak?" (2 Cor 11:29). "[Christ's] power is made perfect in weakness" (2 Cor 12:9). From the perspective of the Cross, anxiety is fruitful, and from the Cross, all the world's anxiety, mediated through the travails of the children of God and sustained by the sighs of the Holy Spirit, becomes the anguish of bringing forth the new world (Rom 8:19–27). The ultimate meaning of the anguish experienced in the contraction of the birth canal becomes clear: it is a subjective feeling of narrowing during an objective process of expanding, in accordance with the paradox expressed in Psalm 4: "*In tribulatione dilatasti mihi* [when I was in distress thou hast enlarged a place for me] (Ps 4:2, Vulgate). As the definitive sign of this paradox, in the middle of the last book of Sacred Scripture, the portent appears in heaven of the great birthgiver, who, crying out in the anguish of delivery, brings forth the Messiah— and then, through all the ages that follow, bears his brethren as well (Rev 12).

II

THE CHRISTIAN AND ANXIETY

In the transition from the Old to the New Covenant a twofold change occurred. First, the phenomenon of anxiety was sharpened to the utmost degree and thus its greatest intrinsic conflicts were clarified. Second, through the vicarious anguish of his Passion, Christ redeemed, subdued, and gave meaning to all human fear. When, in the pages that follow, we speak of the Christian's relationship to anxiety, we must proceed from this accomplishment and these presuppositions found in God's Word and not lose sight of them as the subject develops. Hence this second chapter forms a narrower circle set within the larger circle of the theme of the first chapter.

The first thing that must be said, and which can never be said powerfully and triumphantly enough, is that human fear has been completely and definitively conquered by the Cross. Anxiety is one of the authorities, powers, and dominions over which the Lord triumphed on the Cross and which he carried off captive and placed in chains, to make use of as he wills. In the Old Covenant, too, there was a powerful command: "Fear not!" But this command was challenged in various ways within the process of revelation: by the finiteness of the region illuminated by grace, by the fact that the grace that had been granted was characterized by hope for what had not yet arrived, by the incomprehensible threat of darkness breaking into the region of light despite the guarantees, and finally by man's relapse again and again into sin. Christ removed both the finitude of grace and its modality of hope when he tore down the dividing wall between heaven and earth (by his Incarnation), between earth and the netherworld (by his salvific suffering and his descent into hell), and between the chosen people and the unchosen Gentiles (by his founding of the Church) and when the Father established him as the light of the whole world and the king of all three realms (Phil 2:11). Thereby every reason the redeemed might have for fear has been invalidated. The "world", which as a kingdom of darkness stared Christ in the face at his coming and yet was "conquered" by him (Jn 16:33), has no more claim on the Christian. Neither can any of the "elements of the world", those ancient "principalities", "powers", "rulers of the world", and whatever else Paul may call the known and unknown principles of the created cosmos, in whatever dimension they may be and however they themselves may be disposed toward Christ their Sovereign—neither can any of these be cause for anxiety. And "the last enemy to be destroyed", death, is not exempt from this victory (1 Cor 15:26), nor is the devil himself who "now", in the tribunal of the Cross, has been "cast out" (Jn

12:31)—those twin powers which until then had held the sinner in unbreakable bonds and of which he could only be afraid. From one end of the New Covenant to the other, from the "great light" that dawns in the Gospel to the final victory of the Logos in the Apocalypse, we hear of this subjection and dismantling of all worldly powers under the Son of God, who was chosen from all eternity to be their king. And since this lordship has been entered upon once for all, and the Victor merely "waits until his enemies should be made a stool for his feet" (Heb 10:13), anxiety too has been banished and overcome once and for all. And this is so not merely in a juridical sense and by rights, but, for those who belong to Christ, ontologically and essentially. Insofar as he possesses the life of faith, the Christian *can* no longer fear. His bad conscience, which makes him tremble, has been overtaken and girded up by the "peace of God, which passes all understanding" (Phil 4:7). On Easter day Peter *can* no longer fear the One whom he has betrayed three times. His anxiety has been taken away, and confident love has been granted him in its place. John knows this most profoundly: "[although] our hearts condemn us . . . , God is greater than our hearts, and he knows everything" (1 Jn 3:20): he knows about the love he has poured into the erring heart through the Holy Spirit, a love against which all the self-accusation of the sinner cannot prevail: "Lord, you know everything; you know that I love you" (Jn 21:17). The sinner surrenders; he no longer has any hope of countering, with something of his own or with anything else, the abundance of this hope that has been granted to him.

And thus in the writings of Paul and John, the two greatest witnesses of the Christian life after the Passion, all worldly and obscure regions are totally flooded by the light of God, in whom—in stark contrast with the God of the Old Covenant—there remains no darkness at all (1 Jn 1:5). For John this light is so tender and sweet, for Paul it is so triumphantly resounding, that it can transform even the final anxiety, the fear of the "terrible day of the Lord", into bright confidence: "In this is love perfected with us, that we have confidence for the day of judgment, because as he is so are we in this world. There is no fear in love, but perfect love casts out fear. For fear has to do with punishment, and he who fears is not perfected in love" (1 Jn 4:17–18). "Jesus Christ . . . was not Yes and No. . . . For all the promises of God find their Yes in him" (2 Cor 1:19–20); "in whom we have boldness and confidence of access [to God] through our faith in him" (Eph 3:12), "for God has not destined us for wrath, but to obtain salvation through our Lord Jesus Christ, who died for us" (1 Thess 5:9–10). If, however, those who live by faith need not fear the God who judges, then how much less should they fear any power subordinate to him, whether it be the power of sin, which, alongside death, reigned in the world before the redemption (Rom 5:12–14), or all sorts of "affliction" that the world can, must, and will prepare for believers. Both the Sermon on the Mount (Mt 5—7) and the commissioning discourse (Mt 10) contain Christ's strict command to his followers not to fear, despite all sorts of affliction, even if worse comes to worst. Not a hair of their heads will be harmed. When they step out of the fiery furnace, no smell of fire shall be upon them (Dan 3:27). And the "fear not", which the Lord repeats like a refrain between each of his prophecies of persecution (Mt 10:19, 26, 28, 31), reaches its climax in the jubilant song of praise that is to resound from the midst of the fiery furnace: "Blessed are you when men revile you and persecute you and utter all kinds of evil against you falsely on my account. Rejoice and be glad, for your reward is great in heaven, for so men persecuted the prophets who were before you" (Mt 5:11–12). Beatitude not only is possible under pressure, when one is objectively "in dire straits" ("anxiety" in fact is derived from *angustiæ*, narrowness, straits), it is required. This is the blessedness of Paul: "We rejoice in our sufferings" (Rom 5:3); "With all our affliction, I am overjoyed" (2 Cor 7:4); this is the beatitude of all the martyrs, who went singing to their deaths.

If the Christian's fearlessness before God, before the world, and before every power other than that of Christ is strictly commanded in the New Covenant, it follows that all the "facts" set forth by modern philosophy and psychology concerning the dominance of anxiety are struck down by this command. At first this sounds grotesque, and modern man will say that this prohibition by no means eliminates the fact of anxiety from the world. The Christian can only counter by insisting that "facts" do not eliminate the command forbidding its presence [*Da-sein*]. If it is true that anxiety—about being in the world, about being forlorn, about the world itself, about all its supposedly or really unfathomable dimensions, anxiety about death and anxiety about perhaps inescapable guilt—lies at the root of modern consciousness; if it is true that this anxiety is the basis of contemporary neuroses and that this anxiety is supposed to be overcome through a modern existentialist philosophy by entering into it and affirming it and enduring it with determination to the very end, then to all of this Christianity can only say a radical No. By no means does a Christian have permission for or access to this kind of anxiety. If he nevertheless is a neurotic and an existentialist, then he suffers from a lack of Christian truth, and his faith is sick or frail. Because *this* anxiety has been forbidden by Christ, he has no reason to be afraid with the fearful, perhaps in order to become more like them, the better to understand and counsel and save them. "Brethren, we are debtors, not to the flesh, to live according to the flesh" (Rom 8:12)—and how should our becoming fleshly and worldly help others to conquer the flesh and the world or to go beyond them in the spirit? The sickness of secular anxiety in all its various shadings grips humanity today; even without a (forbidden) firsthand experience, this is easy enough to understand, both in its causes and in the conditions and consequences that follow from it. To heal this sickness, one does not have to suffer from it oneself; on the contrary, only the example of the healthy man can offer help to the sick man. Thus it was in early Christianity, when the new Christians strode through the existentialism of decaying antiquity without contracting it and demonstrated to the infirm the strength of a life that draws on quite different sources and resources. Thus it will be today as well. And if the world's "present hour" makes it harder for people to keep themselves free from anxiety and neurosis than it was in other times, then it follows from this, at best, that more is required of this generation than of others, which probably means that there will be fewer genuine Christians than at other times. Fewer men and women who, with the matter-of-fact courage of faith and by its power, step out into life and lay hold of what God has to offer them: this vocation, this Christian mission, this risk without which a man gains nothing noble, this responsibility, this purity. Against all this today neurotic anxiety is opposed, and as a result so many Christian vocations—which always demand a fearless Yes to grace—are ruined in these times. As a result, today's Christianity is criticized for its tepid, insipid mediocrity. "What a cringing Christianity," the old Bernanos exclaimed, "the world awash with humility beneath its proud airs, but a perverted, degraded form of humility that is nothing more than spiritual laziness and a lack of courage." Only a Christian who does not allow himself to be infected by modern humanity's neurotic anxiety—even though it tries to transfigure itself into the centerpiece, indeed, into the real treasure of existence, even though anyone who does not adore the image of this beast is excluded from the commerce of the anxiety experts (Rev 13:17)—has any hope of exercising a Christian influence on this age. He will not haughtily turn away from the anxiety of his fellow men and fellow Christians but will show them how to extricate themselves from their fruitless withdrawal into themselves and will point out the paths by which they can step out into the open, into faith's daring. But not one whit, either theoretically or in practice, will the Christian stoop to compromise. He will know that "anxiousness" belongs among the things the Lord has forbidden (Mt 6:25–26), that guilt is not the fate of a Christian, and that, through Christ, death has lost its sting (1 Cor 15:55).

Only when this is established unambiguously and irrevocably, adamantly and trenchantly, can one go on—really advancing along the same path, under no circumstances going back or turning aside. Christ has borne the anxiety of the world so as to give to the world instead that which is his: his joy, his peace. But precisely what is his. And this is absolutely inseparable from his earthly life, from his Cross and his descent into hell, and from his Resurrection. All grace is the grace of the Cross. All joy is joy resulting from the Cross, marked with the sign of the Cross. And Cross means anguish, too. When sin-anxiety in all its forms (which comprises everything that throws a person back upon himself, closes him off, constricts him, and makes him unproductive and unfit) has been fundamentally removed from a man and hence has been forbidden him, then from the Cross opens up something completely different: grace, and, in the measure granted by grace, permission to suffer anxiety as a share in Christ's anguish. It is evident how thoroughly this grace revalues anxiety, starting at its basis, and even turns it into its opposite. For if the anxiety of man who is closed in on himself and isolated amounts to a constriction and a loss of communication, then the anxiety granted from the Cross is, on the contrary, the fruit and result of a communication: it is an expansion, a *dilatatio* of the love found on the Cross. As such, it in turn can produce nothing other than a broadening in the person who participates in it. This is not to maintain that the objective opposition will be entirely visible within the subjective experience. It can even happen that, for the sake of an authentic participation, both the participation itself and also its fruit and its structural opposition to sin-anxiety must remain hidden from the person experiencing it. For now we are speaking only about the objective structure of this participation, reserving for later a more in-depth discussion of the laws governing how it is applied, appropriated, and experienced. There is an objective basis to the sin-anxiety that is forbidden to the Christian, and in that anxiety the properties of sin delineate themselves: a turning away, flight, a rigidity of life, sterility, desolation, the plunge into the abyss, constriction, incarceration, withdrawing into self, banishment. In contrast, the basis for the anxiety of the Cross is nothing other than the love of God, who takes this entire world of anxiety upon himself in order to overcome it by suffering, a love that is in all respects the opposite of the sinner's experience of anxiety: it is instead a turning toward, an availability, life, fruitfulness, security and support, expansiveness, liberation. The first set of properties appears as a function of the second. This is true to such an extent that these properties, as anxiety that is *borne*, are not like a compact bundle that is moved externally while remaining unaffected inwardly; rather, the properties in and of themselves, and even as they are experienced, undergo a profound transformation. The change in the structure of anxiety is as far-reaching as the change in the structure of death and of suffering in general. This is already evident in the fact that genuine Christian fear can spring from courage alone, just as the Cross itself of the Son of God sprang from his extreme courage in braving as a solitary man all the powers of hell. The courage of the Christian, which can be loaded with anxiety, is in turn nothing other than his act of faith, in which he dares to place himself and the whole world in the hand of the One who can dispose of him for death and for life.

In the Gospels the anxiety of Jesus' women friends can serve as a paradigm for this Christian anxiety. Their friendship with the Lord and their conduct toward him (Jn 11) prove that they believed with a perfect faith. Their anxiety is imposed upon them directly by the Lord, who, in response to their urgent prayer that he come and help them, remains silent and delays so as to give Lazarus time to die and to allow them time to fear, "so that the Son of God might be glorified". Bereft of their dearest earthly good and in their deprivation seemingly abandoned by their beloved in heaven, the sisters are like the suffering Job, whose anxiety reaches so far into the New Testament. And yet this burden of anxiety (laid upon them as a participation in the Cross even before this had been endured! laid upon the members even before the Head had suffered!) is profoundly different from the anxiety of Job, because it is anxiety within incarnate love; anxiety in patient, albeit uncomprehending, surrender; anxiety without rigidity or rebellion; anxiety without pathos: drawn directly from the fountain of the anguished Lamb who opens not his mouth as he is led to slaughter. Everything reminiscent of Job's argument with God about the law, all the stormy questions—the Why? and the How much more?—fall away; all that remains is readiness and trembling without seeing. Even more characteristic is the fact that this anxiety is laid upon the women in the midst of their concern for their neighbor. Job is alone because it is not possible for him to relate his suffering to any other person. The sisters are isolated in the midst of an all-embracing concern for their dying brother and to an even greater extent for the Lord, whom they serve as human beings and as Christians: their existence is defined by this active and contemplative service. And this service rendered to the Lord, which is the starting point of their anxiety, has been a service of joy. From their joy in the Lord they have been led to share with the Lord a concern for their neighbor, and this shared concern leads to shared suffering and shared anxiety.

It can be formulated as a law that New Testament anxiety is always and fundamentally a catholic anxiety, in which the boundaries of the individual are transcended and blurred, with respect both to the origin and to the goal and effect of anxiety. Ever since the Lord's expiatory suffering on the Cross, in which he made the anxiety of each and every sin—indeed, the oneness of the whole world's anxiety—merge into the oneness of his anxiety as God-Man, an isolated penance for an isolated, personal guilt is, for a Christian, no longer conceivable. Any form of penance, even if it is penance for a particular offense, is Christian only if it has passed through the Cross and received there the form of the universality and indistinguishability of the individual. Otherwise it would still be Old Testament penance (merely of this world), in which the relationship between individual guilt and individual atonement can be calculated within a conspectus of justice. Christianity's core concept is found in the Lord's "new commandment" to love one's neighbor as oneself, indeed, more than oneself, since no one has greater love than the one who gives his life for his friends (Jn 15:13), yes, even for his enemies (Rom 5:10). Therefore Christian anxiety can have its inception only in a loving concern for one's neighbor, whether friend or foe. As the believer leaps into God, he cannot thereby renounce solidarity with his neighbor and leave him to his fate. His leap of faith, rather, must snatch up his neighbor and bring him along; he ought to leap for his neighbor, representing him in an indissoluble fellowship of salvation. The commandment of love does not just go for a few steps. Since it is proclaimed in the face of the Cross and its vicarious suffering, it demands a total engagement, the willingness to go along on the path one is forced to travel (Mt 5:41), to the point of hanging with the other, even unto hanging in the other's stead (Rom 9:3). Christian joy in its totality wells up from this point of solidarity; a joy limited to considering one's own grace and salvation could not claim to be Christian. Christian anxiety springs precisely from the prolongation of this Christian joy: this happens at that point within the mystery of vicarious atonement where something of what Paul yearns for is realized— "[being] accursed and cut off from Christ for the sake of my brethren" (Rom 9:3). Love offers itself in an unabashed trust, indeed, in a blind credulity that be-

lieves with childlike insouciance in every miracle that
the grace of God will work to save the world. Once
the offer is made and the door of finality has closed
behind it, then love's eyes have only to be opened to
what the world's sin is in reality, that is, before God
and before the Crucified One, in order to plunge that
love into an abyss of anxiety. Now an absolutely superior power, an imponderable weight, stands opposite complete powerlessness, an individual who now
only suffers. The miracle has been concealed behind
the dispassionate reckoning of divine justice, and, according to a divine arrangement, the believer is invited to experience some share in the infinite incongruity of the Cross. This is at stake at the moment, and
not a happy confidence that someone else has already
accomplished everything and that every fear has been
overtaken, for that would neutralize the "share [in the]
sufferings" of Christ (Phil 3:10). Consequently, the
anxiety-causing incongruity presents itself as the disproportion between one's own exhaustive engagement,
one's utmost efforts, and the burden of sin and guilt
they cannot even move. This disproportion, which is
absolutely pervasive, cannot help but call forth absolute fear. The miracle of Christian trust in God and
in the redemption on the Cross is something delicate,
something that can be made intelligible and believable
only from heaven's perspective, so that it takes merely
a breath to cover this clean mirror with the cloudi-
ness of anxiety. Trust and hope seem so improbable

that the anxiety that springs from them—precisely at the point where God takes them seriously—appears almost probable and normal in comparison. And if God often and even in most cases spares the believer anxiety, then one must discern in this a new, as it were, intensified grace of the Cross. Nevertheless, the anxiety of the Cross is not such that it at any point doubts faith, hope, or love in its absoluteness, despairs of their operation, sets itself in opposition to these three, or makes the salvation that has been accomplished yet is always being accomplished seem unreal, questionable, or ineffective. Although subjectively the fearfulness of the Cross can lead one quite close to such an opposition, it never crosses over the threshold. And since objectively it is a mode of faith, love, and hope, a phase of their fulfillment, a process within their vital interior space, Christian anxiety can be portrayed only as a mystery in which faith, hope, and love overlook their own presence, indeed, renounce any further recognition of themselves. This eclipse and alienation belong to the deed accomplished by the crucified Son, his act of giving over to his Father in trust all of his own strength and vision, so as to be able to suffer in complete deprivation. The Son has not relinquished what was his as though he were now to possess the opposite characteristics, but rather in such a way that, for the moment and "until further notice", what is his has become inaccessible and hypothetical for him and, therefore, without force or effect. He has renounced everything so categorically that any grasping at it, any effort to help himself with it, is entirely out of reach. All of that may exist, the bright realm of faith, love, and hope, but in his anxiety he is excluded from it; for him it is out of the question. And since he has really and with utter seriousness renounced the consolation of this light, he does not see either to what extent it can be possible for others. To know that, to be certain of that would be the summit of blessedness for someone who is genuinely suffering. He who *wants* to suffer must rob himself of the use of this knowledge. And he who *must* suffer in the grace of the Cross will be robbed of his. Thus the eclipse of faith, love, and hope in their own characteristic fulfillment is the exact opposite of their eclipse through sin, when one falls from their midst or entirely out of their realm. In Christian anxiety the image of God in the soul is veiled to itself, just as images in a church are during Passiontide; in sinful anxiety the image of God itself is damaged or destroyed. The former is a heightening of Christian truth, a proof that God counts a soul worthy of his most precious mysteries; the latter is a lessening or loss of truth, a proof that a soul has wandered away from God's world.

Accordingly, a *first law* describing Christian anxiety can be formulated as follows: *Christianity is intent upon and capable of delivering man from sin-anxiety, provided that he opens himself up to that redemption and its conditions. In the place of sin-anxiety, it provides him with anxiety-free access to God in faith, love, and hope—which, however, be-cause they stem from the Cross, can in and of themselves put forth a new, grace-filled form of anxiety that stems from catholic solidarity and shares in Christ's work of atonement.*

But now this first, simple line is crossed by a second one that threatens to confuse its clarity again. For the crucified Son of God, who is sinless, the opposition between salvific anxiety and (to him inaccessible and unproductive) sin-anxiety is self-evident. And it is also comprehensible that something of this salvific anxiety can be communicated to a believer out of the superabundant grace won on the Cross. But do not Christians, even as redeemed, believing, loving, hoping Christians, always remain sinners? Whether they fall back into grave sin and then perhaps, just as the Apostle warns, sin much more horribly than an ignorant heathen (Heb 6:4–8); or whether they struggle in the twilight between love and lust, hope and faint-heartedness, as "half-saved souls" whose basic direction remains uncertain, who again and again merit the description "sinners" just as literally as the description "the just"? Certainly a human being cannot simultaneously possess sanctifying grace and be someone who hates God, in the sense in which Luther or the *Heidelberg Catechism* have interpreted the phrase "*simul justus et peccator*". But how much truth this phrase still contains for anyone who knows or suspects his weakness, his perversity, his constant backsliding, his hopelessly lukewarm attitude, his profound failure to correspond to the Lord's commandment! Faced with his own shameful compromises, this being neither hot nor cold, will not a new anxiety seize him, a fear that is quite understandable yet comprehensible only to a Christian, the anxiety of an impossible Both-And, which is therefore a Neither-Nor? And is not this, perhaps, the specifically Christian anxiety, or at least the kind most frequently encountered and the one which, by its ambiguity, betrays itself over and over in the most painful way to the outsider, the unambiguous/unequivocal heathen? If "these redeemed folks ought to look more redeemed", if these Christians do not come across convincingly, then one reason is the uncertainty born of an uneasy conscience over doing their job so badly and failing to be a credit to their cause. Another, even more lamentable reason is their fear that others might see through them and perceive that they in fact are not at all what they claim to be.

At this point Christian anxiety seems to relapse into the Old Testament. There anxiety could be overcome by virtue of the promise; but because what was promised was not yet present, it lacked the strength to wrest man completely away from sin-anxiety. The suspense between the sinful present and the promise that could never be made fully present became the birthplace of a new form of anxiety. In the middle of the New Covenant this seems to repeat itself: inasmuch as the accomplished salvation remains eschatological and the sinner is still journeying toward perfect righteousness, then to some extent the twilight between "fear and hope", or, to put it more clearly, between the sinner's fear of God and of condemnation and the believer's hope for salvation, will never be completely illuminated. Does not the New Testament foster this twilight by strengthening both the promise and the threat and making them definitive? Yet, in so doing, which requires anyone who stands in its force field to endure a superhuman tension (to fear in earnest and to hope simultaneously, to be certain yet to leave everything in suspense), has it not overstrained the human soul by winding its powers too tightly? Is it feasible to live within this contradiction? Or do these contortions prove that something impossible has been asked of man in this instance? Does not the Christian who takes sin and salvation seriously get lost in a dialectic with no exit, in which each increase in grace brings forth an increase in unworthiness, even guilt, so that in this tangled thicket religion becomes the real inferno? And does not all this furnish the most merciless psychoanalysis with an easy target?

It cannot be denied that something like vertigo can come over a man, even a believer, in this transitional state between fear and hope; after all, it is a routine fact. But Christianity cannot be blamed for this loss of footing; it has to be laid at the door of the man who does not want to take Christianity seriously. Christianity offers man, not a bottomless pit, but solid ground —grounding in God, of course, and not in self. To

place oneself on this solid ground involves relinquishing one's own ground. The sinner wants to stand on
his own, not on God. And whoever tries to stand both
on God and on his own is sure to fall into the bottomless space in between. The realization, or even just the
experience, that one is standing in this bottomless pit
presupposes that one has stopped walking—walking
on God's ground or making the passage from one's
own ground to God's. Living, efficacious faith means *to
walk*, to be under way. Everyone who walks has ground
under his feet. Faith, love, hope, unceasingly offered to
man, are the ground that is constantly being pushed off
under his feet. Sin refuses this ground in order to take
a stand on one's own; yet even between sin and the
repentant return to God, speaking now as a Christian,
a momentary loss of footing does not necessarily inter-
vene. Whoever believes, whoever reaches out for faith,
takes a real step, and while he steps he cannot simultaneously philosophize about the possibility of stepping,
cannot reflect introspectively upon the passage from
himself to God and have it in his grasp. In the first
place, that would be a contradiction, and the outcome
of such reflections could be nothing other than contra-
dictory, merely verbal dialectic. From a Christian perspective, once there is a possibility of passing over to
God (and God makes this possible by grace), the job of
mastering this passage, still from a Christian point of
view, is no longer in man's hands. When man is really
walking, God has already provided for the possibility

of walking and solved the problem of continuity, and so all the paradoxes of the mind, about Achilles and the tortoise, are passé. The uneasy conscience that many Christians have, and the anxiety based on it, do not come about because they are sinners and backsliders but because they have stopped believing in the truth and efficacy of their beliefs; they measure the power of faith by their own weakness, they project God's world into their own psychological makeup instead of letting God measure them. They do something that Christians are forbidden to do: they observe faith from the outside; they doubt the power of hope; they deprive themselves of the power of love; and they lie down to rest in the chasm between the demands of Christianity and their own failure, in a chasm that, for a Christian, is no place at all. Is it any wonder that anxiety seizes them on account of this placelessness?

Thus there is no such thing as a Christian reflection on some static relationship between the anxiety of sin and the anxiety of the Cross. The law of exclusion rules between them, a law that can be defined only in terms of the movement from one to the other, a genuine movement, a firm stride—in the same way that faith is described in the New Testament as something tangibly sure, giving rest and security—certainly not as a flickering dialectic between sin-anxiety and assurance of salvation, trembling before the devil one minute and triumphing over him the next. Somewhere around here Luther missed the mark, however unfath-

omably profound his knowledge of Christian anxiety
may have been otherwise. Luther had to arrive at his
dialectical solution, because in his concept of salvation
he abided too closely by the Old Testament understanding of promise and eschatology and because he
was unwilling to accept either a real deliverance from
the anxiety of sin or a real participation in the anguish
of the Lord's Cross. In the Old Testament as well these
two existed either not at all or only in the form of
promise. And so this Neither-Nor had to turn eventually into a dialectical Both-And, while the interest
of the theologian, preacher, and pastor was necessarily
redirected toward that impossible In-Between which
is forbidden to Christians. This in turn, in a genuine
continuation of the Lutheran dialectic, inevitably led
to the Kierkegaardian concept of anxiety: the vertigo
of the finite mind when faced with itself, with the
rupture between the finite and the infinite that it finds
within itself, with its own unfathomable freedom. Everything that Kierkegaard expounds—with such dialectical depth!—regarding the reciprocal causation of sin
and anxiety only goes to prove that he is lingering at
a level of thought for which there is no provision in
the Christian scheme of things. This level is neither
the naïveté of Adam's belief nor the fearlessness pre-
scribed for the Christian as he strides along toward
God; instead, as Kierkegaard correctly perceives, it is
the level of a psychology, which in and of itself is not
dogmatic theology. Within this psychology, *because* it

is not dogmatics, dialectical anxiety is at home. It is characteristic of Kierkegaard's Lutheranism to the nth degree that the fundamental anxiety for him is not (as in Calvin's scheme) an anxiety before the judgments of divine predestination, but rather the anxiety of one faced with the abyss of his own mind. Kierkegaard becomes thus the connecting link and transition between Luther and Heidegger.

But Calvin, too, came to a standstill in making this transition. He too stopped and reflected at the point where faith is required to take steps and advance. As a result, the two-sided character of divine judgment, which can be explained only by *laying hold* of the faith, disintegrated into the theoretical system of double predestination. Here a new, unchristian anxiety necessarily builds its nest, at a different place than in Luther, but just as fundamentally. This time the relapse into the Old Testament lies in the profoundly individualistic notion of man's salvation that excludes any ultimate solidarity. Wherever limited salvation surfaces in Christian thought—Jansen will underscore this notion yet again—anxiety is on the drawing board, too. The history of French Jansenism and its aftereffects down to our own day is virtually nothing but a chronicle of the devastation wrought by this anxiety.

These ways of thinking are forbidden to the Catholic. He cannot, by means of some dialectic, calm the person who despairs of or just plain doubts the reality of his passage to God; on the contrary, he can do so only by calmly pointing to his living faith as the real step taken in this passage. To be sure, to make such a gesture is also the basic intent of both forms of Protestantism. But the vertigo of reflection that seizes them prevents the aspect of present reality from becoming effective alongside the eschatological aspect. The Catholic cannot view salvation merely as an objective fact accomplished on the Cross, which the believer then notes together with its effect; rather, between objective and subjective redemption he sees the requirement of participatory appropriation. Consequently, the path from sin-anxiety to redeeming anxiety is for him a real pathway. If he strides toward the latter, the former can only lie behind him; if he draws closer to the latter, he distances himself simultaneously from the former. Between the two, separating them, necessarily lies the zone of fearlessness, indicated by the radiance of faith, love, and hope. Only at one point does something like a "dialectic" come into play in Christian redemptive anxiety as well, and at this delicate, easily injured point misunderstandings and misinterpretations will arise again and again: the believer who is drawn into the grace-filled anxiety of the Cross can never see himself as being in a unity with the Redeemer over against sinners. Such a direct and unbroken unity would be false and objectionable on both objective-theological and subjective-experiential grounds. No Christian stands on any sort of equal footing with Christ in matters of justification, and no one who is drawn close to him by grace is tempted to mistake himself for Christ. Precisely at the point where grace calls him "friend", he acknowledges himself to be "servant", and not merely servant but sinner. On the way of the Cross Christ alone is the victim; anyone else in the vicinity either is being justly crucified for his sins (like the two thieves) or is someone guilty of Christ's crucifixion (and that he is in any case). All real and objective participation in the Lord's anxiety on the Cross can, subjectively, have only this fractured character, which distinguishes the anxiety of a Christian from the anxiety of Christ and marks the abyss between them, for he who suffers here by grace is still a sinner who has inherited original sin. This is not to say that his sinfulness is expressly presented and explained to him as the cause for his anxiety; to the contrary, it may remain concealed from him just like whatever deposit of supernatural light he must leave in trust with God. But even in that case, he will never be tempted to mistake his anxiety for that of the Lord; rather, he will endure his anxiety in the lonely place allotted to him, in an obedience that is incomprehensible even to him.

Therefore by way of summary we can enunciate a *second law*: *Insofar as we are sinners and even as believers can always become sinners anew, the anxiety of sin is not simply taken away from us by the objective act of redemption on the Cross but rather is set before us even in the New Testament. We are permitted to leave sin-anxiety behind us to the degree that we appropriate in truth the living faith offered to us from the Cross, that is, a faith active in our lives. However, even when the grace of sharing in the anxiety of the Cross is granted, the distance between the one who suffers in compassion and the Redeemer who originally suffered is maintained in its entirety, and the anguished soul is aware of it.*

A third point is already implied by the preceding, although it should still be brought to light explicitly. If the anxiety that participates in the Cross is a special fruit resulting from the gift of faith, love, and hope and is a particular, God-granted intensification of this Christian gift, then it is impossible for a human being to be led from the anxiety of sin directly into the anxiety of the Cross. In other words, the theological locus for the mystery of the obscurity in the anxiety of the Cross is necessarily found within the comprehensive mystery of Christian redemption from sin and from sin-anxiety, consequently, within Christian joy. A genuine participation, as God has intended it, in the dark night of the Crucified can occur only as an episode between one light and the other, between one joy and the other, between one strength and the other. It is not only improbable but intrinsically impossible that God would lead a human being who has never experienced the full glory of Christian serenity [*Befriedung*] right from the anxiety of sin into the anxiety of the Cross. This is true especially of the mystical night in the strict sense, which, being distinctively Christian, can be interpreted only from the perspective of the Cross. It is not primarily a phenomenon of "purification" that would be situated somewhere toward the beginning of one's spiritual journey; rather, it should be understood primarily as a Christian and thus as a social grace which is administered exclusively by God and therefore can be conferred at any stage in the spiritual life—the only restriction being, of course, that it is granted only to the one who has come to know God's light in faith, love, and hope in the very depths of the soul. For such a "dark night" is nothing other than the privation of *this* light, and the more profound the antithesis, the privation is, the more complete and effective the night becomes. Only the Son of God, begotten from all eternity in the bosom of the Father and nourished by his essence, can fathom to the utmost what it means to be forsaken by the Father. Again this is illustrated by the women of Bethany: they could not have felt such anxiety at the incomprehensible absence of Jesus had they not been his friends, had not the bliss of his presence been for them the quintessence of life. If this is true of the great mystical night, and of the great mystical anxiety that occurs in it, then it is valid by way of analogy—in a smaller format, as it were—for every Christian life of faith that is alive: the "consolation" of faith always precedes the "desolation" that follows, because this trial, as a *Christian* tribulation, could not be experienced at all except in the withdrawal of a spiritual light.

This must be taken as a warning above all by the Catholic writers who undertake to portray Christian anxiety. They assume thereby a heavy responsibility, the more so to the extent that their testimony carries weight within and outside the Church. Someone who associates with Georges Bernanos for any length of time will not be able to maintain the objection that so easily arises from a passing acquaintance, namely, that he exaggerates the dark night and the despair and the anxiety. A glance at his life, which rushes from one catastrophe to the next yet consistently bears the mark of Christian authenticity, will quiet any lingering doubts. Beyond all the tendency to grandiloquence and all the tumultuous passion (no less vehement than that of his spiritual ancestor Léon Bloy) lies the region from which his work springs: unerring assurance in matters of the Church and of the supernatural, which he unveils with the businesslike touch of a physician who desires neither to sensationalize nor to falsify anything but only to show what is there. From his childhood on, Bernanos himself knew anxiety, for it dogged his footsteps and never let him go as long as he lived. But it did not impede his uncommonly triumphant and chivalrous courage; indeed, it was ultimately only a form of this courage: to be naked and defenseless before God, like the saints he portrayed. And so in the year of his death he was able to thrust through to a depth at which the words describing his agenda are neither exaggeration nor blasphemy:

We really will what he wills. Without knowing it, we really will our suffering, our pain, our loneliness, where of course we think we will only our joy. We imagine that we flee our death, while we really will this death in all truth, just as he willed his. As he offers himself on every altar where Mass is being celebrated, so he begins his death anew in every man who lies in mortal terror. We want what he wills, but we know not what we will, we do not know ourselves, sin makes us live on the surface of ourselves, and we will only come home to ourselves to die. And he awaits us there.

Gertrude von Le Fort's novella *Die Letzte am Schafott* [*The Song at the Scaffold*] is more questionable, not on account of its portrayal of mystical anxiety and of the sacrifice offered therein, in extreme weakness, nor on account of the juxtaposition of this "small weakness" with the virile heroism of the novice mistress, who, as it turns out, is not among those destined for the sacrifice. Rather, it is more questionable on account of the manner in which a natural and congenital anxiety in the character of Blanche de La Force, one could even say a decidedly neurotic anxiety, is supposed to constitute the basis for mystical anxiety, or, at any rate, the seamless manner in which one turns into the other. Blanche's anxiety is a matter of "disposition" and is linked to her having been born in the midst of a panicked mob. "At an early age she displayed a timidity that greatly exceeded the little fears one usually observes in children." " 'Are you sure the stairs will not

slip from under my feet? . . . Won't the wall tip over?
Are you sure the gondola will not sink? Won't people
get angry?' " the girl asks constantly. Later she finds
"little devices to mask the true state of affairs. . . .
[Blanche] would suddenly feel tired or ill, she had forgotten to learn her lesson or to fetch something she
needed. In short there was some reason or other why
she could not set foot on the stairs or in the gondola."[1]
Her entry into the Carmelite convent at first is clearly
a flight from anxiety into safety, and in the midst of
this neurotic anxiety and "fear of fear", a vocation to
genuine mystical anxiety overtakes her. Now, there is
no reason why such a calling could not befall a fearful
character just as well as a naturally strong and fearless character. But precisely for that reason one should
not establish a continuity between the two anxieties,
indeed, the appearance of such a continuity must be
removed explicitly, by showing how the light and sure
strength of the vocation separates these two very different kinds of darkness—the natural-neurotic anxiety
and the supernatural anxiety—from each other.

If the beginnings of the vocation to anxiety are du-
bious in Gertrude von Le Fort (although at the end,
under the scaffold, the light breaks through), in Paul
Claudel's *L'Otage* [*The hostage*], the end of the heroine,
Sygne de Coufontaine, is shrouded in extreme dark-

[1] *The Song at the Scaffold*, trans. Olga Marx (New York: Sheed and
Ward, 1933), 10–11.

ness. After she has sacrificed her honor, the honor of her noble line and, symbolically, the honor of the entire social order that had been based on royalty, so as to rescue the pope, the Church on the brink of the Revolution, amid the gathering storm-clouds of an empty and meaningless liberty, every possibility of forgiveness and joy, every power of peace within her has been completely exhausted. She dies with the "nervous tic" of shaking her head and saying No, not by way of contradicting the truth, but because she has not even an ounce of strength left to say Yes. The destiny and actions of Claudel's characters are always determined by the symbolism contained within them (most pronouncedly in his *L'Annonce faite à Marie* [*The tidings brought to Mary*]). What is alarming about his art is that, although the symbol (the downfall of the *ancien régime* in the Christian sacrifice for the New) is impeccably precise, the character doing the symbolizing is strained almost to the point of dangerous boundary violations. The three aforementioned writers recognized and took up their standpoint precisely in the intellectual locus of Christian anxiety: in the French Revolution, in the collapse of the entire old world order before the advancing chaos of liberty —understood as chaotic openness and unlimited potential—which, considered from the Christian perspective of openness to God, can only be assessed as a diabolical counterfeit of truth. Yet the sacrifice of the *entire* order (which, after all, is the only one) is demanded: atrociously, extortionately, and so unsparingly as to plunge man into the ultimate anxiety. But in this downfall some things endure: that integrity for which Bernanos is fighting: Hold firm! Be brave! In the death of the young Marquise de La Force the invisible power of the Cross endures, capable of shaping an unforeseeable future: "The Revolution is over. In fact, the reign of terror collapsed ten days later." Even the honor of Sygne de Coufontaine endures despite all her disgrace:[2]

SYGNE: Come with me where there is no more sorrow.

GEORGES: And no more honor?

SYGNE: Neither name nor honor.

GEORGES: Mine is intact.

SYGNE: But what is the use of being intact? The seed that one plants in the earth. What good is it unless it decays? All earth is the same six feet under.

Reinhold Schneider knows well: "There is no revolutionary tragedy. The idea is self-contradictory. The tragedy is that, of all lives, the best and highest life must fall, and that the law in any case is more than life and existence" (*Macht und Gnade*, 30). Yet Schneider knows something more profound—that the collapse cannot merely take place within a firmly established

---

[2] From act 3, scene 2: *The Hostage: A Drama*, trans. Pierre Chavannes (New Haven: Yale University Press, 1917), 137. For the sake of von Balthasar's argument, Chavannes' translation has been rendered more literal. TRANS.

framework, but the frame itself has to break with it, in order to acquire new validity from the sole formative law governing history: the Cross. Within this all-consuming contradiction is found Christian tragedy, as well as Christian anxiety. Here it is that the writer must portray it. But in doing so, how could he forget that under this sign no downfall can be so horrible as to prevent the fire of salvation from breaking even more radiantly through every crack and joint of the crumbling edifice?

Hence, in the portrayal of great Christian anxiety, one must very carefully and vigilantly see to it that its intrinsic laws, which are determined by the Cross, stand out in sharp relief: its remoteness from natural fearfulness, its origin in the certainty and joy of Christian mission, and its culmination in the victory of the Cross. It is even more important to maintain clearly the boundaries delimiting Christian anxiety from sin and from sin-anxiety. Even a great writer like Graham Greene or a work like Gertrud von Le Fort's *Kranz der Engel* [*Wreath of angels*] cannot be absolved from what Karl Rahner has branded as a false and fatal "mystique of sin", namely, the thesis set forth under the pretext of sincerity and anti-pharisaism, that guilt itself, when assumed voluntarily (in solidarity with another sinner), contains a redemptive element, which is today perhaps the decisive element; this plainly and necessarily contradicts true redemption. Though the framework of a Christian individualism, a speculation about one's own

salvation that contemporary man feels to be egotisti-
cal, may burst irrevocably (and it is good that it does),
the laws of the gospel are still unscathed and remain
unshakable for each generation. In God there is no
darkness, and in guilt there is no light. The Son of
God became like us in all things except sin, and this
"except" is the prerequisite that enabled him to take
each and every sin upon himself and to atone for it
completely. Whoever deviates a hairsbreadth from that
rule entangles everything. A Christian can share bur-
dens and be in solidarity precisely in the measure that
he has separated himself from sin. He can enter into
anxiety on behalf of the sinner precisely in the measure
that he has, objectively, been freed from the anxiety
of sin.

Accordingly, the *third law* will read: *God grants a (mystical or even usual) participation in the anxiety of his Son
on the Cross to no believer unless he has first granted to him
the entire strength of the Christian mission and joy and the
entire light of faith, love, and hope—that is to say, unless
he has first taken from him the anxiety of sin. To consider
a "synthesis" of both to be possible, or even worth striving
for, does not conform to sound Christian doctrine.*

III

THE ESSENCE OF ANXIETY

As we go back down to the question of the essence of
anxiety we do not leave the theological realm behind;
rather, as we seek to understand more deeply what has
been revealed, we bring to bear whatever our reason is
capable of contributing to the subject. In other words,
we make use of philosophy, so long as this is understood to be what it is and what it alone can be: the
reflection of the human mind on the first principles
and causes of this concrete world. As revelation shows
us, this world was never a "purely natural" world, but
rather one created by God within the ambit of supernatural grace and ordered to a single supernatural
end: the contemplation of God. Even in falling away
from him the world has not become a "purely natural"
world but remains in every respect nestled in the supernatural. Thus the object of philosophy is from the
outset something more than philosophical (if one considers grace and revelation as belonging to the specific
object of theology), particularly since human reason,
which is both object and instrument of philosophical
work, never was or will be any more "purely natural" than the "nature" from which it arises. So little
basis is there for such a claim that one can go ahead

and postulate and formulate the concept of a nature entirely separated out from the supernatural, but the lack of adequate data from experience and observation makes the constructive development of such a concept impossible for the philosopher. Nature as we know it is the nature that is moved and moving between the Fall and redemption, intrinsically affected by both modalities to such a degree that not even the speculative reconstruction of the original nature in paradise (which as a real "state" stands even closer to nature as it now exists) is possible without contradiction, let alone a never realized state outside of any relationship to the supernatural. As long as the philosopher resigns himself to this restriction imposed upon him by revelation, denying him a field of endeavor that would be fully independent of revelation (because there is no "grace" without "revelation", since the ontological and epistemological sides of God's supernatural self-disclosure are intimately connected), the contribution of philosophical reflection within theological investigation is most welcome, indeed, indispensable. After all, what else should the science of theology use to build itself up if not the reflective labor of reason?

Therefore this work yet to be accomplished is not exclusively a matter of further and more fundamental analysis of the biblical texts as such; rather, in the light of what is revealed in them, it is a matter of analyzing human reason and human nature insofar as they are affected by that light. For revelation expressly invites human reason and nature to think about and understand themselves anew within the declarations and predications issued by the Word of God. A wide-open field is allowed for this activity: human reason can legitimately bring forward its own findings in order to see what becomes of them in the light of God's Word, to determine to what extent they stand and to what extent they are to be rejected, or to what extent they are, after a suitable recasting, finally applicable: *intellectus quærens fidem*. Reason can likewise start with the Word of God, so as to import it (the expression of the concrete order of being as it is manifested by God) into the order of being that man can grasp from his own vantage point, and to acknowledge this Word as the final, absolute truth of the relative truth heretofore belonging to him: *fides quærens intellectum*. Anyone wishing to make a cleaner separation here would sever the vital ligaments of truth.

Since Plato, philosophy has designated *admiratio* [wonder] as its fundamental act, in which reason, stepping out of its everyday routine, catches sight of the existing thing as such. It did not require a Heidegger to discover how close this fundamental act is to anxiety. The relationship of wonder to astonishment is already found in Plato, indeed, one might describe this transition as the most intrinsic characteristic of the Socratic genius, inasmuch as Socrates incessantly discloses something seemingly familiar to be unfamiliar (thereby arousing astonishment), only to make it, from this distance, truly recognizable for the first time (so that it causes wonderment), but also inasmuch as he demonstrates that something apparently unknown is in truth something recognized. The effect of estrangement involved in being surprised is simply a function of the deeper, admiring eros. Thomas Aquinas sees the reciprocal relationship between these two forms of wonder when he raises the following objection: "The philosophers are moved by *admiratio* [wonder] to inquire for truth, as [Aristotle] says at the beginning of the *Metaphysics*. Fear, however, moves one not to inquiry but rather to flight. Therefore *admiratio* is not a form of anxiety" (*S. Th.* I/II, q. 41, a. 4, obj. 5). In his response, however, Thomas distinguishes three forms of anxiety, insofar as it is brought to the mind by an external evil. Such an evil can exceed man's power of resistance (and thereby arouse his anxiety) in three ways: first, on account of its magnitude, when its dimensions are indeterminate, in which case it produces wonder (*admiratio*); second, on account of its unusual and improbable character, in which case it produces a numb bewilderment (*stupor*); third, on account of its unforeseeable character, in which case it produces dread (*agonia*). Thomas replies to the objection as follows: "He who wonders (*admirans*) shrinks from passing judgment on that at which he wonders, since he fears failure—but in the future he inquires. However, he who is benumbed in perplexity fears both to judge in the present and to inquire in the future. Hence wonder (*admiratio*) is the beginning of philosophizing, but perplexity is an impediment to philosophical examination" (*S. Th.* I/II, q. 41, a. 4 ad 5). The distinction is artificial but does point back to the close connection between wonder and astonishment that led Hegel, Kierkegaard, and Heidegger to declare dis-composure [*Ent-setzen*], vertigo, angst to be the fundamental act of philosophy, that is to say, of the mind in general. In so doing, they preferred anxiety, with its movement of flight, to hope, with its movement of trust. These two, fear and hope, have been opposed to one another in their definitions from time immemorial. The object of hope was described as "a future good that is difficult but possible to attain (bonum futurum arduum, quod quis potest adipisci)", and the object of fear as "a difficult future evil that cannot easily be avoided (malum futurum arduum, quod non potest de facili vitari)" (*S. Th.* I/II, q. 42, a. 3, *resp.*; *Summa contra gentiles*, I, 89). Yet hope's movement of trust includes, together with the concept of attainability, the whole subjectivity of striving and of what is "good for me", whereas the distancing movement of anxiety actually excludes this subjectivity and thus creates the free space in which the thing can emerge in its objectivity. (So too in theology, the *via negativa* has from ancient times been regarded as more objective than and hence superior to the *via positiva*, because it seeks to determine God's attributes, not from his relations to the creature, as in the latter method, but rather in God himself, absolutely, by distinguishing him from the creature.) Wonder—the enthusiastic ardor for the sublimity of being, for its worthiness to be an object of knowledge—promises to become the point of departure for genuine insight only where it has reached the stage in which the subject, overwhelmed by the object, has, as it were, fused into a single point or into nothing. (To supply again a clarification from theology, this is like the movement of hope and love toward God, which is genuine and selfless only where it has assumed the attitude of pure worship of God for his own sake.) This point, at which subjectivity is overwhelmed by the object purely in itself and all of the wishes and strivings that color one's vision are set aside by the untroubled, majestic realism of its quiddity, its being-so-and-not-otherwise, is also the point of anxiety. What is essential to anxiety is the suspension of the reassuring balance of forces between subject and object and, thus, a kind of exposure of the subject to the object ("timor est de futuro malo quod excedit potestatem timentis, ut scilicet ei resisti non possit" [*S. Th.* I/II, q. 41, a. 4, *resp.*]).

If one inquires into the object, the about-what of anxiety, ancient philosophy distinguishes two kinds of evil about which anxiety is anxious: "Aristotle says (*Rhetoric* 2.5) there is the fear of destructive evil (evil that undoes being [*malum corruptivum*]), before which nature recoils because of its natural desire for being, and such fear is called a natural fear. And alongside it there is the fear of distressing evil [*malum contristativum*] which does not conflict with nature but with the desire of one's appetitive faculty, and this kind of fear is not called natural" (*S. Th.* I/II, q. 41, a. 3, *resp.*). The first corresponds to a threat to the substance, the second—a danger to the activity (*S. Th.* I, q. 48, a. 5; *Contra gentiles* III, 6). The quintessence of the natural threat is death, whether it be a "natural death" resulting from natural causes or a "violent death" resulting from an unnatural cause. And yet, Thomas continues, following Aristotle, this natural threat must occupy a particular position in order to be an object of fear: neither so distant that the thought of it is too faint to arouse immediate anxiety ("all know that they must die, but because death is not near, they are unconcerned about it" [Aristotle, ibid.]) nor so near that the onrush of disaster buries anxiety beneath it ("those about to be beheaded have no fear, faced with the inevitability of approaching death" [ibid.]). "On the contrary, a certain likelihood of escape must be present if one is to be fearful" (*S. Th.* I/II, q. 42, a. 2, *resp.*). To elaborate: there must be a certain open space in which the threatening menace can maneuver at all: pressing forward from an inconsequential distance up to the edge of oppressive proximity, as well as rushing back from tangible immediacy into a receding, sinking distance.

This is where the ancient philosophy of anxiety reaches its limits. It has spotted on the horizon the total threat to substance posed by death. But it has described the fear of this threat as conditioned, as limited by a certain proximity and distance. Corresponding to this delimitation is the classification of anxiety among the *passiones animæ*, which, in their proper and strictest sense, mean suffering by loss, something that can happen directly only to a material being. "This means that *passio* in the proper sense can reach the soul only indirectly (*per accidens*), that is, insofar as the composite (of spirit and body) suffers" (*S. Th.* I/II, q. 22, a. 1, *resp.*). Accordingly, *passio* is shifted more to the appetitive than to the cognitive faculty, and more to the sense appetite than to the intellectual appetite (the will) (ibid., art. 2–3). Therefore, according to Thomas, the threat to nature or substance, which produces natural fear, can apply only to physical death (and thus to the separation of the soul from the body, the dissolution of the "composite"); it can never threaten the being of the creature as a whole. The soul's consciousness of its immortality and thus of its invulnerability to the *malum corruptivum* of nothingness is so powerful, and medieval man's confidence in being is so great, that an anxiety of the sort that would cast doubt on finite, creaturely being does not come into view at all. Even then, such an anxiety would not be primarily a *passio* (in the sensitive part of the soul), rather, it would be a behavior of the intellectual soul as such, or of the mind, insofar as it, being finite, sees its limits and in seeing transcends them. It is here, where the threat to the finite mind (which, being spiritual, still possesses a certain endlessness) calls into question the mind as a whole and not merely its corporeal side, that we first find the connection with the Old Testament anxiety that trembles before the paradox of the finitude of the salvific region, which nonetheless harbors the infinitude of salvation. The impetus for this was given by an era during which confidence in being was profoundly shaken, an era that consequently transferred anxiety from its peripheral place as a *passio animæ* to a central place as a "fundamental situation" of the finite mind.

Then it became apparent—though the Middle Ages had already caught sight of it—that the complete sensorium allows no room for anxiety in the proper sense, because it does not comprehend directly or in itself the dimension of the future from which the threat approaches. It follows that an animal can have only a natural-objective and not a subjective relationship of fear to the thing that threatens it ("sensus non apprehendit futurum, sed ex eo quod apprehendit præsens, animal naturali instinctu movetur ad sperandum futurum bonum vel timendum futurum malum" [*S. Th.* I/II, q. 41, a. 1 ad 3]). The sense faculties can, of course, be "startled" when something to which they are accustomed is missing, but they cannot actually wonder and thus cannot become anxious. The sensorium is a finite and compact framework of apprehension, which can receive only what it is set up for: tones, lights, colors, and so forth, within a finite range of perception. Too loud a noise or too harsh a light will be "shuttered out" by the sense organ itself. At the limits of the capacity for perception there may well be an indeterminate zone in which a certain extension is possible through practice and stretching, accompanied perhaps by pain, but this prolongation of the finite gamut by no means implies a surmounting or a transcendence, such as would be required for a radical questioning or a total threat. Thus the fear of an animal remains a phenomenon completely distinct from the mental anxiety that is our sole concern here, even though ancient philosophy was, on the other hand, correct to view human anxiety not as a merely intellectual but as a psychosomatic phenomenon, that is, as a phenomenon that comprehensively involves precisely the mind in its finitude.[1]

The locus of anxiety in the mind is indicated by the reciprocal relationship between transcendence and contingency. Transcendence means that, for the mind to be capable of recognizing an existing thing [*ein Seiendes*] as such, it must have surmounted each individual and finite existing thing and have caught sight of Being [*das Sein*]. But Being is neither finite nor an existing thing, rather, it is that by which an existing thing is in existence. Therefore it does not have the character

---

[1] This is not the place to discuss in detail the question of animal fear. A better understanding of it would require taking account of what Thomas has to say about the "interior senses" in *S. Th.* I, q. 78, a. 4. Cf. Karl Rahner, *Geist in Welt* (1941) [*Spirit in the World*, trans. William Dych (New York: Herder and Herder, 1968)].

of an object, either; it is not presented like a thing to the mind in its act of cognition; rather, just as it is the ground or reason that an existing thing *is*, so too it is the ground in the mind that enables it to recognize an existent as such. Of itself, Being is indifferent as opposed to this or that, since Being can be everything. Hence the mind that wishes to know individual existing things must let itself become as unrestricted as Being itself in its indifference, so that from such a perspective it can get the measure of every difference. The mind needs to have within itself a stage that is empty and so large that all things can appear and play their roles upon it. One cannot say that this emptiness is simply "Nothing", since it is the negation of the existing thing only insofar as it is the constitutive Being of all that exists. Yet one cannot call it "Something" either, for this is the designation for the existing substances and their relations and qualities. Neither can one call it the genus of all that exists, since it transcends such a concept to an infinite degree and qualitatively: the positing of an infinite number of existing things neither defines nor limits nor even gradually exhausts Being as such; untouched in its transcendence, it remains what it always was—that through which an existing thing is in existence. This transcendence, which has been named the ontological difference, is at the same time the expression of contingency, which cannot be grasped any more precisely than by ascertaining that no individual existent and no aggregate of existing things is ever Being and, therefore, that Being never appears and realizes itself as such in any existent or in any collection of existing things.

The yawning gulf in the midst of transcendence and the contingency manifested therein is grounds for anxiety for the mind as it comes to know what exists. In every act of cognition the mind must relinquish and lose its footing in existing things and align itself with Being—in which one can never become firmly established [*Boden fassen*], because it is incomprehensible [*unfaßbar*]—so as to be referred then back from Being to the existing thing. Being is not a category or a concept; it is that by which the mind, letting go of everything, must itself be apprehended in order to comprehend something. The anxiety in the innermost essence of cognition lies in the fact that knowing takes place *between* two poles, both of which as such necessarily elude knowledge: Being eludes knowledge because it can never be an object of cognition; rather, it remains the prerequisite for all objective knowledge— just as in Plato's allegory of the cave the light behind the prisoners is a condition for their seeing the shadows but is itself never seen. The individual existent eludes knowledge because it would really be known only if it could be placed in an intelligible relationship with Being, by which it is the way it is in all its parts —only, I say, if it could be derived from Being and proven to stand in a necessary relationship to it. Both are impossible. Cognition has to be suspended between the two; accordingly, within the ontological difference found in indifference with respect to Being, cognition must allow Being to differentiate it in ever-new ways in relation to existing things—without ever attaining to Being itself through indifference or ever reaching the necessary quality of the existent through differentiation. Although one cannot say that Being is related to the existent as the universal is related to the particular (since every particular thing is such through Being, and since Being, consequently, stands beyond universality and particularity, grounding both), still the ontological difference is nowhere more impressively mirrored than in this relationship. The immense chasm that yawns between the universal and the particular is for the mind, in its act of cognition, the indication and the constant reminder of the deeper, often forgotten gulf between the existent and Being. Here the question facing cognition becomes urgent and even almost brutal: Why does it encounter precisely this particular thing and not another? How could the facticity of these facts, both individually and collectively, ever be explained based on the system of universal laws? The sum total of what is actual can never be rendered intelligible as the necessary articulation of a world of ideal norms, nor can the norm be understood as the mere empirical formula for the factual behavior of things. If thinking should ever be naïve enough to believe one or the other and to set itself in motion accordingly, sooner or later it will be struck by the brutal force of the contingency that reports its presence in this gulf: where the factual is so thoughtless and dull in its occurrence, while the law set over it is so indifferent and without effect, that the incongruity of the existing thing's composition causes the gulf to yawn immediately between the existent and Being. Is this concrete human being whom I encounter supposed to embody the idea—undoubtedly glorious —of man? And if he cannot and if most human beings are incapable of it, how can the idea of man as a generality act as the norm for such a humanity? To put it differently: If I am a man because everything that belongs to the idea of man is realized in my essence —including uniqueness—how can this idea of man be indifferent with respect to my uniqueness and realize itself (always indifferently) in millions of other human beings? If I am indifferent with respect to the idea (if my humanity is interchangeable with that of another), then the idea is not genuinely embodied in me, unless indifference belongs to the idea, which, however, eliminates the notion of personality. All the woven artifacts of meaning that experience and science establish and trace between facticity and the norm (and who would deny that they are endlessly varied and exciting) are actually hanging unsupported, with no way to connect either end, within the void of the ontological difference. It is a void because thinking not only sees that it is not filled but understands that it cannot be filled. As long as the universal is what thought necessarily recognizes it to be, it cannot manifest itself exhaustively in the facts. And as long as the existent is what thought necessarily recognizes it to be, it cannot claim to offer a full and complete image of Being. Hence one will not say that the existent as such, even in its restrictedness, is a cause for anxiety; but it becomes such a cause when it is considered in its relation to Being —and every act of cognition puts it in this relation. There is just as little truth to the statement that Being as such, even in its unrestrictedness and incomprehensibility, is uncanny for conceptual thinking, but this it is in its relation to what exists, which for cognition is the only expression of Being, though not a necessary one. The mind that stands outside in transcendence in order to know what exists cannot help wondering whether it is *worth* the effort expended—indifference with respect to all that exists—if it thereby gains real knowledge neither of Being (which never becomes objectified) nor of the existent (which can never be deduced from Being), and this because the gulf yawns in the very structure of objectivity.

The young person who leaves behind the child's immersion in particular existing things and emerges into the sphere of the comprehending intellect and of transcendence experiences for the first time enormous *disappointment* with the world. The more intellectual and spiritual he is, the more profound his disappointment. The transcendence opening up to him appears at first to be something enticing, an invitation to all sorts of adventures like the awesome "descent to the [arche-

typal] mothers" in the second part of Goethe's *Faust*.
Eventually, though, he realizes that the path does not
lead *toward* any place, but rather leads *back* unexpect-
edly to the particular again, and that this path was intended as a cognitive method of knowing better the
particular in the world. And yet from this point on-
ward, because the vista of transcendence has opened
up, the particular can no longer have the weight of
an absolute, as it did for the child; somewhere along
the route the particular has become indifferent. In formal terms, transcendence is that which makes thinking
possible in the double movement of *abstractio* (the abstraction of Being from the existent) and *conversio ad
phantasma* (the projection or reading of Being into the
appearance). In terms of content, however, this double
movement is the drawing away and uprooting (*abstractio*) of the mind from its familiar environment into the
unfamiliar horizon of Being and then its return to the
world, which now becomes visible for the first time in
its character of being an appearance (*phantasma*), resulting from its contingency and un-familiarity. The *exces-
sus*, the *ekstasis* (ἔκστασις) of thought beyond sensation
conceals within itself the first beginnings of anxiety—
not because a larger space opens up, but because this
space, which makes conceptualization possible, is still
inadequate to offer a satisfactory interpretation of the
objective world, indeed, precisely because this yawning ontological difference rules out such an interpretation. The same structure that reveals the truth of

Being also veils it; the same structure that causes the light of Being and of the agent intellect (*intellectus agens*) to dawn also spreads to the same extent the night of meaninglessness and incomprehensibility. In the ontological difference the world becomes abstract in two directions: the existent loses some of its importance inasmuch as it is seen as the appearance of Being, and Being gains nothing in importance inasmuch as it is dependent upon this existent as its appearance. Abstractness becomes the *inner quality* of worldly being and of the secular mind, a quality that is falsely explained in epistemological terms as phenomenalism (for we are not denying things their existential quality: the point is to characterize this very quality) and which maintains neutrality vis-à-vis a more idealistic or a more realistic philosophical approach. The ontological difference gives to worldly being an abstract-ghostly outline which the mind, insofar as it stands in the middle of the difference during the cognitive act, can register in no other way than as anxiety.

This becomes much more evident if one considers the mind no longer as reason but as will. Now the indifference of the intellect toward Being-as-such, which was the prerequisite for knowledge of any differentiated existent, appears as the indifference of the will with respect toward Being-as-such, which is requisite if any particular being is to be freely chosen as a good. On the one hand, Being-as-such (since it is not an object) cannot be chosen by the will, just as it cannot be known objectively by the understanding. On the other hand, openness to Being-as-such is the prerequisite that enables the will, out of the remoteness of the mind, and thus in freedom, to choose a particular good at all. The same thing that removes (sensual) necessity from the will and transforms it from a blind drive into a superior intellectual faculty of choosing is also what forces upon it an indifference that includes a certain lack of concern with respect to all worldly goods. Under this pressure the will finds itself to be free, since no choice obtrudes itself with serious finality. What is called free choice (*liberum arbitrium*) contains inseparably within itself this positive element of a distance freed from compulsion and this negative element of serving as an arbiter between various parties or viewpoints, of which it can be stated a priori that no one of them is right in an absolute, totally compelling sense. And so once more, the absoluteness of an abstraction from the concrete (in order to be able to choose at all) is out of proportion to the purpose of the abstraction: the choice of something that is always contingent anyway. Herein lies the real "vertigo of freedom" faced with its own infinite, indeterminate and unfathomable character, which can become vertiginous only because this "possibility" is counterbalanced by no actuality, that is, no necessary character in the object-to-be-chosen. Once more, it is not our purpose in making this point to undermine true ethics and advocate relativism. But the best moral calculus and abstract hierarchy of values with the surest formulas for choosing cannot relieve the will of its fundamental anxiety of being elevated in the first place to the dizzyingly exposed position of an arbiter and judge (*liber arbiter*).

Now the question arises: What is this human nature we have been describing thus? Is it the essence as God created it, the "first nature", or is the structure we are examining here defined by that difference from primordial nature, from the original creative intention, which we call the "Fall" and "original sin"? If we assume that the latter is the case, then God did not create anxiety as a component of nature, and all of the distance or remoteness within nature (as it became evident in the description of the ontological difference and its reflection in intellect and will) would be partially determined, in its concrete reality, by the distance of the sinner from God, by the falling dynamic of guilt. Partially determined, and not simply determined, because from another perspective the ontological difference is by necessity the very expression of creatureliness itself, in whatever state the creature may be. But partially determined in such a way that the modality of transcendence and contingency as we have sketched them could not be explained otherwise than through a falling away. In that case, one would be compelled to bring the abstract component in the mind into a closer connection with the theological truth of the fall into sin. The void that opens up in the mind, the cause of its anxiety, could then be traced back to an absence—

and whose absence, if not that of its Creator and grace-giver, the "sweet guest of the soul" who had chosen it as his dwelling place?

Though we may hesitate to follow through with the consequences of this idea for human knowledge, because what philosophy has presented from time immemorial as the structure of discursive thought seems inseparable from human nature as such, it does seem possible, even unavoidable, to follow through when we ponder the free will of the creature as it comes forth from the Creator's hand in original grace. Kierkegaard is right: "To maintain that freedom begins as *liberum arbitrium* . . . that can choose good just as well as evil inevitably makes every explanation impossible."[2] To begin with the *liberum arbitrium* as one's point of departure is to presuppose something that cannot legitimately be presupposed with certainty: the knowledge of good and evil, or, what amounts to the same thing, the pernicious neutrality and indifference toward good and evil, with respect to God and anti-God. God did not set his creature in this bad position; indeed, the whole point of the prohibition in paradise was to preserve his creature from it. The prohibition was meant to preserve man from the lukewarm place between hot

[2] *Begriff der Angst* (Jena, 1923), 111 [*Concept of Anxiety*, trans. Reidar Thomte and Albert B. Anderson (Princeton, 1980), 112], cf. 44 [49]: "However, freedom's possibility is not the ability to choose the good or the evil. Such thoughtlessness is no more in harmony with the Scriptures than with thought. The possibility is to *be able*."

and cold, the place of not having decided for good
against evil—or even simply for the good, without
knowing or suspecting evil, but being turned toward
God alone and therefore turning his back on all that
is not encountered in turning to God. The beloved
good that is totally present to the lover relieves him
of all choice: he is the one who is decided, who has
no other choice, and who experiences therein his entire freedom and liberation. We are not saying that
Adam saw God face to face, for if that had been true,
his subsequent falling away from God would be in-
explicable. We are only saying that the space within
Adam that became a place of emptiness and indifferent
freedom through the withdrawal of the divine presence was a space that God had originally created for
himself and had filled with his mysterious and, on the
other hand, unquestionable presence. It was a presence
in faith, naturally, but it occurred in a now no longer
attainable obedience and love that possessed and em-
braced God immediately and with childlike certainty.
A faith for which God, though not seen face to face,
is the most present, *most concrete* reality, whence all that
is substantial in the world receives its equally certain
and unquestionable rightness, obviousness, and name-
ability. In the evening breeze of paradise God walks
and talks with Adam: invisible, yet as tangible and all-
pervasive as the wind. In him we live, and move, and
have our being. And from this life Adam draws his
royal but still not tyrannical dominion over the realm

of nature, which, with every step he takes, opens itself up to him in its concreteness at that moment. And so it is understandable that the older theologians, including Thomas Aquinas, ascribe to Adam, besides "discursive" thought, an intuitive thinking ability, which one would have to understand less as "infused knowledge" than as a knowledge arising from the concrete life of faith in God. Since Adam is a creature, the dimension between the universal and the particular, between the existent and Being, subsists for him, too. But no void yawns between either of these tensions, because both the universal and the particular, both the existent and Being itself are for him transparent toward God, who, standing beyond both of them, grants that he may be known in both.

The transition from this life in God and with God to a life in sin requires, as Kierkegaard shrewdly noted, an "intermediate term" [*Zwischenbestimmung*]. This necessarily involves the ambiguity that, on the one hand, it leads over into sin and is a prerequisite for sin, but, on the other hand, since it leads to sin, it can stem only from the realm of sin and must have sin as its prerequisite. Kierkegaard understands this "intermediate term" as anxiety, which is latent at the basis of innocence and ignorance, insofar as the slumbering mind dimly senses in its depths the endlessness and possibility that are awakened in it by the boundary of the prohibition. "In this state there is peace and repose, but there is simultaneously something else, though it is not contention and strife, for there is indeed nothing against which to strive. What, then, is it? Nothing. But what effect does nothing have? It begets anxiety. This is the profound secret of innocence, that it is at the same time anxiety. Dreamily the spirit [= mind] projects its own reality, but this reality is nothing, and innocence always sees this nothing before it."[3]

Man is a synthesis of the psychical and the physical [that is, soul and body]; however, a synthesis is unthinkable if the two are not united in a third. This third is spirit [the mind]. . . . [The] [mind] is present, but as [an] immediate, dreaming [mind]. Inasmuch as it is now present, it is in a sense a hostile power, for it permanently disturbs the relation between soul and body, a relation that indeed has permanence and yet again does not have permanence, inasmuch as it is still to receive permanence by the [mind]. On the other hand, [the mind] is a friendly power, since it is precisely that which constitutes the relation. . . . [The mind] is afraid of itself. The [mind] cannot get rid of itself; nor can it lay hold of itself so long as it has itself outside of itself. . . . Flee away from anxiety, it cannot, for it loves it; really love it, it cannot, for it flees from it.[4]

---

[3] *Ibid*. [English trans., 41.]

[4] *Ibid*., 38; [pp. 43–44]. (Terminology has been modified for consistency with HUB's argument. TRANS.)

Kierkegaard operates here with the categories of Romanticism and of German Idealism. Although his intention is Christian, he so emphasizes the relation of the spirit to itself that he runs the risk of forgetting the main point: the relation to God. This is, to be sure, connected with another fact: Kierkegaard does not admit that Adam is qualitatively different from the rest of mankind. Vehemently rejecting the "state of original justice", he banishes it to the realm of myth, which ruins theology. Consequently, Adam's state before sin is not qualitatively different (although it is quantitatively different)[5] from that of every man in the ignorance and innocence of unawakened consciousness.

> The individual is both himself *and* the race. This is man's perfection viewed as a state. It is also an antithesis, but an antithesis is always the expression of a task, and a task is movement. But a movement whose goal is the very thing which had been first assigned as a task is a historical movement. Hence the individual has a history. But if the individual has a history, then the race also has a history. . . . Every individual is essentially interested in the history of all other individuals, just as essentially as in his own. Perfection in oneself is therefore the perfect participation in the whole. . . . As the history of the

[5] Emil Brunner, *Der Mensch im Widerspruch* (1937) [*Man in Revolt*, trans. Olive Wyon (Philadelphia: Westminster, 1947)] goes so far as to deny even the quantitative difference between Adam and every man. ["Jedermann" is an emblematic figure from a German medieval morality play; thanks to an English translation, "Everyman" has acquired some of the same connotations for those who have studied humanities.]

race moves on, the individual begins constantly anew (because he is both himself *and* the race), and in him so does the history of the race.[6]

If one wishes to do justice to the truth expressed in these statements without surrendering the Catholic doctrine concerning the original state that Kierkegaard rejected, two possible paths are open. The first is the one taken by Josef Bernhart (*Chaos und Dämonie* [1950]), in which the original state of nature, as well as every subsequent concrete state, converges to the extent possible with nature as such (*natura pura*) and the privileges of Adam are reduced to a minimum, while the proclivity to sin (*Versuchlichkeit, peccabilitas*) of original nature and the danger to it are emphasized as much as possible. He thus finds himself on paths taken by the oldest and best-documented tradition of the Church,[7] according to which the finite mind can attain the full actualization of its destiny only by passing through a choice and a temptation. Thus, the state at the outset of his path may indeed be good and sinless, but it is a state that can only be indifferent with respect to the decision that has to be made for the good. From here a second path opens up, one that, with Gregory of Nyssa,[8] defines the original state dialectically, as ideal

[6] *Ibid.*, 23 [28–29].

[7] See Henri de Lubac, "Esprit et liberté dans la tradition théologique", in *Surnaturel* (1946), 187–321.

[8] See our study *Présence et pensée: Essai sur la philosophie religieuse de Grégoire de Nysse*, 2d ed. (Paris, 1988) [*Presence and Thought* (San Francisco: Ignatius Press, 1995)].

and reality simultaneously. In this dialectic, the *reality* of the original state (in the tradition starting with Irenæus, which Bernhart also invokes) can be considered as the sole possible good of the beginning (which, in this respect, is a complete good that does not fall short of the idea of man). Viewed, however, from the perspective of the *ideal* intended by God for man (as in the tradition of Origen), this reality can only be regarded as an initial prerequisite for the subsequent history and drama of the decision. This gives us the right to view Adam's relation to God as an ideal one, in comparison with which every relation to God after the temptation and Fall is to be regarded as deficient; at the same time, though, it also gives us the right to view the ideal as a reality established in Adam's coming forth from the creating hand of God (coming forth in the latency of unknowing innocence, but in an innocence that is nonetheless real)—a reality that stamps all subsequent falling away with its genuine, abysmal character of deficiency. Thus both are true: that one cannot begin (realistically) apart from the free-will decision in indifference (as de Lubac and Bernhart, together with the Fathers and the Scholastics, maintain) and that one nonetheless may regard the indifference that has been realized, and the emptiness and anxiety that gape within it, as an alienation from the real origin even before the actual Fall into sin took place.

As for the essence of anxiety, it follows that Kierkegaard identified its point of origin correctly but did not sufficiently describe, with regard to its content, the vertigo caused by the void that opens up within the finitude of the mind. The mind is made anxious, not by the void of nothingness in its own interior dimension, but by the void that yawns wherever the nearness and concreteness of God have withdrawn into a distant estrangement and have yielded their place to "someone over there", to an abstract relation to an "other".[9] What brought man from a state of neutrality and indifference to such a position vis-à-vis God that man presumes to arbitrate between God and anti-God? This is ascribed to the influence of the serpent, that is, of evil plain and simple, and it therefore belongs to the sphere of ungodliness. It is not so that, as long as man stayed in the nearness that God had created, he was susceptible to temptation based on a "creaturely anxiety" about being able to fall. Nor is it so that God, withdrawing and leaving the void behind on purpose, put man in a position to be tempted. But God had to leave open to man the space that made it possible for man to move away. And God could not spare man the experience of being tempted by what God had excluded and forbidden, which precisely by being forbidden acquires its power over man.

Once this space has been entered, anxiety is the order of the day, and because Adam "is himself *and* the

[9] See Romano Guardini, *Welt und Person* (1940) [*World and the Person*, trans. Stella Lange (Chicago: Regnery, 1965)].

race", the space can no longer be closed and anxiety can no longer be banished. From now on, anxiety is intrinsic to the mind on the basis of the gaping void in it, but this immanence has a transcendent prerequisite: alienation from God. Thus "Nothing" is the proximate basis for anxiety, but the nothing that makes anxiety anxious is not simply the nothingness that pervades finitude as such, the mind's inner transcendence and contingency. Rather, what makes anxiety anxious is the awareness of a fundamental falsehood, displacement, guilt—an awareness called forth by the absence of the One who ought to be present in this "Nothing". Philosophical ontology, when it analyzes the concrete consciousness of man, can grope its way very close to the origin of anxiety. The undeniable connections between the most formal structures of the mind in thinking and willing and the concrete historical reality of man's condition lead forward to oppressive obscurities, which, however, are illuminated in the presence of revelation. And the analyses of philosophy, once they allow revelation to lead them beyond themselves, acquire their own helpful significance.

Anxiety has arrived on the scene with the void, and Christ's redemption does not eliminate this void. His redemption, to be sure, brings God's fullness, but it conveys it into the form of this void. It is said of the Redeemer that he emptied himself and made his way into the void. The void is thereby filled, to be sure:

God is there. But he is no longer there in the way he was present in the evening breeze of paradise—as that Presence which, for man and his nature, is the most real, in which and through which everything else gains its reality. Instead, God is present as the unfelt fullness, as fullness in the void. In paradise God was the *primum notum* (in faith, not in sight), both *quoad nos* and *in se* [the first thing known, both with respect to us and in himself]. Today he is the *primum notum* only *in se*, no longer *quoad nos*. Abstraction and the indifference of the will are not eliminated; they remain the form in which and by way of which faith's immediacy and concreteness have to actualize themselves. With that we have finally circumscribed the ultimate attitude of the Christian: through the abiding void in man (the *indifferentia intellectus et voluntatis ad omne ens* [the indifference of the intellect and will toward every being]) God's fullness reveals itself as presence in such a way that God as the first thing demands from man a total Yes to his invisible totality and in-difference. This Yes—the living point where faith, love, and hope are one—is in the same way characterized as Christian indifference. It is the surrender of one's own void together with its anxiety into the unfelt fullness (which therefore feels like a void) of God's Totality. That also describes the passage from what human nature (after original sin) is in its innermost essence—namely, indifference as transcendence of every nature-based difference with respect to Being—to what Christian nature is in its grace-based essence, namely, indifference with respect to the God who has become man in this nature. The distinctively Christian act is unattainable to nature, yet it lies precisely in the prolongation and elevation of nature, indeed, in this act all nature joins in accomplishing its own act: to transcend the world and to reach the God who is truly revealed and has drawn near—this accomplishment, though, taking place again in the concealment of the human act tending toward the God who has become man.

Indifference means letting go of the sheltering, supporting difference: stepping out without guardrails. Climbing over the gunwale and stepping out onto the water. Transcending, while trusting solely in what lies beyond, from which the power and possibility of transcending come. The attitude *in which* the act of transcendence takes place is not this power; if that were the case, the power would be finite and differentiated, and by clinging to this attitude, by summoning forth this attitude, by reflecting on this attitude, everything could be bent back out of genuine transcendence into false, philosophical transcendence, into "philosophical faith". The attitude is nothing in the absence of that which makes this attitude possible: God present in Christ. In reflecting on his belief ("How can I be doing this?"), Peter is already back in unbelief and sinks, and within transcendence is uncovered what had been swallowed up and drowned while transcendence was advancing step by step: anxiety. One cannot simultaneously let go and cling to the letting go. Faith, love, hope must always be a leap for the finite creature, because only in that way does it correspond to the worth of the infinite God. It must always mean taking a risk, because God is worth staking everything on, and the real gain lies, not in a "reward" for the daring leap, but in the leap itself, which is a gift of God and thus a share in his infinitude. In the daring leap, something of the limitless self-giving of the Divine Persons to each other becomes visible in a flash—at the point where all ground, which is limitation, is relinquished and where man can actually sense that being in the Absolute means—hovering. Lifted up in the arms of grace, carried on the wings of love, he feels a *tremor*, which, in and of itself, bestows on him precisely the security needed to stand no longer on his own or on the earth but to be able to fly by a new power.

All of this is Christian because it has its archetype in Christ. One cannot say of him that he had faith in the sense that we are supposed to have it. Nevertheless, in a passage that is very often commented upon because it summarizes the entire salvific economy of faith, the Apostle calls Christ the "pioneer and perfecter of our faith" (τὸν τῆς πίστεως ἀρχηγὸν καὶ τελεωτήν [Heb 12:2]), because he has to accomplish the same act as the Christian, only in the opposite direction, as it were. Whereas by venturing to let go of everything the Christian takes a stand beyond finitude and comes into the limitlessness of God, Christ, in order to make this act possible and to be its source, has dared to emerge from the infinitude of the "form of God" and "did not think equality with God a thing to be grasped", has dared to set out into the limitation and emptiness of time. This involved a transcendence and a boundary crossing no less fundamental than that of the Christian, and Christ undertook it so as to entrust himself henceforth within time, with no guarantee or mitigation from eternity, to the Father's will, which is always given to him in the present moment. He is not the one who determines and knows the hour: only the Father has it at his disposal. He permits himself to be led in the same patience (*patientia*, ὑπομονή) that marks the fundamental attitude of the Christian within time, the attitude that, for the Christian, expresses itself as faith, love, hope and as indifference directed toward the Father. In standing outside of eternity and entering into time, the Son of Man has known anxiety and therein, as in everything he was, did, and suffered, he has translated something incomprehensible and divine into human language (that is, after all, what revelation is): God's fear and trembling for the world, for his creation, which is on the verge of being lost. Anyone who tried to object that such a thing cannot be reconciled with God's eternal happiness would have a rather narrow concept of God.

In standing outside of everything so as to place himself unconditionally at the disposal of God's totality, the believer hands over to God, along with everything

else, his emotional disposition as well: faith that loves
and hopes is ultimately indifferent even to anxiety and
nonanxiety. In and of himself he can presume nothing,
hence he must await even this from God. It is God
who, as *absolute* Transcendence, has the creature's anxiety and sense of security at his disposal. If faith is really indifferent, then any anxiety that is placed within
it, as well as the complete dispelling of anxiety in a
shower of consolation and sensible certainty, can only
be a gift granted by God himself. Whatever reasons a
man, as a natural-fallen creature or as a Christian (in
his detachment from the world and in his solidarity
with all others, yet to be redeemed) might have for
being anxious are surpassed by another reason: loving
and hoping faith, which, as such, is indifference to
God. For faith says Yes to every truth of God, seen or
unseen (affirming the latter even more); it says Yes to
the truths that console and to those that do not, to the
truths of divine joy as well as to those of the divine
Passion, and waits for God to dispose and differentiate. Once again the law described in chapter 2 of this
book recurs here: only he who has left the anxiety of
sin behind attains the fullness of faith and thus true
indifference, and the entry into the realm of complete
truth is unconditional joy, consolation, overwhelming
light. When God bestows Christian suffering, including Christian anxiety, it is, viewed from his perspective, fundamentally an intensification of light and of
joy, a "darkness bright as day", because it is suffering

out of joy, anxiety *out of* exultation: it is a sign of God's ever-greater confidence in the one who believes. And what experientially seems constricting and frightening to the believer is in truth enlarging, a fruitful *dilatatio* of the birth canal, an interior trembling that expands faith, hope, and love. Even if subjectively it were mortal terror, objectively it is greater blessedness, a participation in the everlasting trinitarian ecstasy.

Indifference with respect to the God of Jesus Christ corresponds in the supernatural realm to the indifference of intellect and will in the realm of nature to all being. The actualization of supernatural indifference by God, however, possesses two aspects, just like natural indifference: abstraction (all the way to pure Being) and conversion (to the appearing image, to the *phantasma*), or, to put it in Christian terms, detachment from everything (all the way to God) and turning back (with a mission to the world). But just as in the natural process abstraction must precede conversion, at least logically (though not psychologically or temporally)— since otherwise the conversion could never be able to see something existent within the appearance—so too Christian detachment must precede Christian mission (logically, psychologically, and temporally), if the resulting mission is to be genuinely Christian at all and not merely worldly-religious. In the immediate act of judgment that knows an existent and posits and affirms it as such, in the indivisible act of the will that reaches for *this thing* in making the right choice and takes re-

sponsibility for it, certainty is found, and the mind hits
the rock of being. All searching, groping, deliberating,
and consulting has its place either before, in achieving
the judgment or choice, or afterward, in assimilating
what has been judged or chosen. Accordingly, there
is Christian anxiety *before* the mission—at the point
where the soul is being cleaned out—and, if need be,
again while the mission is being carried out (if having
anxiety belongs to the mission), but not in the act itself of being sent: here clarity, certainty, and agreement
necessarily and unconditionally rule. The prophet who
stands before Yahweh can be anxious *before* being sent,
and anxiety can be part of his mission; but at the moment of being sent, anxiety is taken from him without
a trace. The act of sending, which presupposes complete indifference, has and retains for the person sent
something of the character of the rock upon which the
Church rests. She rests, of course, upon the mission of
the apostles and of Peter in particular, but that mission
cannot be separated from the mission of the prophets
of the Old and New Covenants.

On all these pages there has been much talk about
the Christian but little about *the Church*. "The Church
and anxiety" could be the central theme for a new
treatise. Without broaching this subject, we nonetheless must draw attention to the place occupied by the
Church within the theme "the Christian and anxiety".
The Church constantly demands too much of natural
man by asking him to imitate Christ. All of Christian-

ity, as the Church and the Church alone presents it
to men and embodies it for them, will always appear,
and rightly so, to be an exorbitant demand, an exces-
sive strain, and thus a threat to and the destruction of
natural man and his laws and limits. Yet in all of this
the Church's sole desire is that man might dare in faith
to go beyond his own nature, that he might persevere
and live in that leap of faith. Now God has not only
offered man the invisible help of grace to make this
leap, but also, by becoming a visible man and founding the visible Church, he has made accessible to man
an abundance of visible helps as found in the organs
and functions of the Church: ecclesial office and the
men who exercise it; Sacred Scripture as a tangible
word; the sacraments as definite forms and vessels of
the salvific encounter between man and God; tradition,
which enables the believer to align himself with the
past; the example of the saints and of all fellow Christians who have a living faith; the firmly established
order of the Church year, which takes the believer in
and leads him gently from mystery to mystery. These
are but so many supports and handrails with which
to teach and train him for that one leap away from
all handrails. This is the paradox of the Church, but
it is already the paradox of God-become-man, of the
"economy" [of salvation]. This paradox is immediately
resolved when one reflects in faith on how the Father
can be seen in the Son of Man and considers how all
the "means of grace" in the Church are intended to

contain and mediate nothing other than the closeness of the incomprehensible God and of his love. Now it is clear that someone who does not see this paradox and refuses it, who is anxious about the leap of faith, will use all the helps provided for that leap to defend his anxiety from the leap. The Christianity of the Church as such is not a "religion of anxiety"—arousing anxiety through its claims and threats, then numbing anxiety through its forms and rites—but, because existence in the Church is the most vulnerable kind of human existence, everything about the Church is a hairsbreadth away from anxiety, and the naysayer who refuses the risk finds faith and faith's God to be an eternal object of anxiety, and the ecclesial forms to be incomparable defenses for that same anxiety, in a dialectical game that is impossible to disentangle. And certainly a dialectical theologian or a depth psychologist can analyze the Church's "demonic element" more and more deeply and, in doing so, refer to all sorts of husks and encrustations of anxiety with which "men of the Church" have surrounded her over the millennia. But that is to say no more than what we already knew anyway: that the misuse of the best leads to the worst and that the most precious thing is its own protection. This was the teaching of the New Testament, in which the presence of infinite redemption becomes the *reason* why the shadows of hell that gather to oppose it become darker than ever.

Thus it is undeniable that the handrails the Church

offers to the believer and the use the believer makes of them are always in an acute crisis and liable to become ambiguous. We can leave aside the cruder forms, in which man thinks that by dint of a "materialization of grace" he can superstitiously and magically gain power over God and salvation. Consider the more difficult and subtler forms, for example, appealing to tradition in order to avoid the demands of a decision that can be made only in the vulnerability of a unique situation; appealing to the unreasonable proof from probability when it is the improbable that must be done and should come to pass. Or consider the abysmal problem of the relation between God's Kingdom and earthly power (into the ultimate depths of which probably only Reinhold Schneider has the courage to descend today): whether, for example, a call to arms by the Church, a blessing of weapons, or taking up the sword of this world is an expression of the courage of Christian faith or, on the contrary, the symptom of an unchristian and faithless anxiety; whether something that can be defended and justified in a hundred ways with penultimate reasons drawn from faith (quite apart from the lessons of Church history—but then *what* does Church history teach?) will collapse miserably before the throne of judgment of the *ultimate* reason—because what of course appeared to be God's weapon in the hands of God's warrior against God's enemies is now suddenly exposed as Peter's desperate sword-waving against the high priest's servant, whose side Jesus takes in order to expose such brandishing of weapons for what it was: anxious betrayal.

To be a Christian in the Church requires courage. Courage is by no means the opposite of anxiety. It is just as ambiguous a phenomenon as anxiety, running the gamut from primitive and mindless states to the highest faculties of the soul. We are talking here about the Christian virtue of fortitude, which, on the one hand, like all things Christian, is a grace bestowed by God. On the other hand, especially at the point where this virtue seizes a man and thoroughly suffuses him with its glow, it takes up into itself the best, most noble behavior of man. The courage of the mind, at the natural level, is based on a primal knowledge of its own ability, on a sense of itself as a possibility, as a plan drawn up and awaiting realization, and as the capacity to realize it. The radius of this possibility, however, is the same as that of the span or void that opens up within the mind in the acts of knowing and willing. For despite all the vertigo of being ripped open, the mind still knows that this void is *itself*. Even anxiety does not destroy this primal sense; indeed, anxiety ultimately takes its measure from that primal feeling; anxiety can only be the anxiety of this courage itself. This courage becomes natural fortitude at the point where, keeping in view the rational plan of being, namely, law and duty, it does not waver but, resolutely on its path to its highest possibility, endures every situation, every attack, every anxiety. It becomes Christian for-

titude, however, at the point where the plan finds its
conclusion and origin in God himself, so that from
man's perspective (far more than in the ἀπάθεια and
ἀταραξία of antiquity) receptive indifference becomes
the all-decisive criterion: in the form of the courage to
say Yes in every instance to every word of God that
may affect my life. Of all things, defenselessness and,
from the natural human perspective, weakness (and,
last but not least, anxiety) now become the essential
prerequisites for Christian fortitude. Right where I become serious about baring my heart and my life, the
real power (which is not mine but God's) radiates most
purely. "But we have this treasure in earthen vessels,
to show that the transcendent power belongs to God
and not to us." We are oppressed on every side but are
not made anxious; "perplexed, but not driven to despair; persecuted, but not forsaken; struck down, but
not destroyed" (2 Cor 4:7–9), "but he said to me,
'My grace is sufficient for you, for my power is made
perfect in weakness.' I will all the more gladly boast
of my weaknesses, that the power of Christ may rest
upon me. For the sake of Christ, then, I am content
with weaknesses, insults, hardships, persecutions, and
calamities; for when I am weak, then I am strong"
(2 Cor 12:9–10). Ever-increasing defenselessness is an
ever-increasingly open stance toward God and for God,
and hence an ever-increasing influx and indwelling of
God's power in man. No one is as unarmed and exposed as the saint is toward God, and therefore no

one is as ready to be deluged by every anxiety; yet
this is the quintessence of courage and armament—
by God. But it is not as though the brave man who
is defenseless toward God should appear to the world
only like a Saint George bristling with weapons. It is
true that any courage he may have in facing the world
derives from his being armed by God. But the "armor
of God" that Paul tells the Ephesians to put on because
he wants them to be "strong in the Lord and in the
strength of his might" consists in nothing other than
"truth", "righteousness", "faith", "salvation", and the
"word of God", which are to be "armor", "belt",
"breastplate", shoes, "shield", "helmet", and "sword"
for the Christian (Eph 6:10–11, 13–17). To put it even
more succinctly: "Put on the breastplate of faith and
love, and for a helmet the hope of salvation" (1 Thess
5:8), that is, arm yourselves with those three things
that together mean the soul's one openness to salvation. In this openness, which the Christian possesses
and allows to radiate from him like a light, he conquers
the self-contained, armored world. In this world, however, he is not abandoned but is placed in the Church.
And inasmuch as the Church represents God to him—
concretely in her office and in her love for *these* men—
his openness to God becomes in him an openness to
the Church; it becomes ecclesial obedience. That is the
decisive test of whether his courage is Christian, for
"the Mameluke, too, shows courage." On the other
hand, inasmuch as the Church is a fellowship of those

like him, the weapons of God work in her and upon her in the same manner as they will later harden and sharpen themselves in confronting the world. Not in the manner of compliant lackeys and subalterns, but on the contrary: as courage to discern the spirits, to speak plainly, to do the deed that not "everyone" is doing, to wield the flashing sword that again and again severs chaos as at the beginning. Christ's "flock" is never at any time Nietzsche's "herd"; being in the Church is based on choice and decision. For all his gentleness and humility unto death on the Cross, God does not relinquish his attribute of being judge and consuming fire. Nothing is more majestic than his Passion; even his anxiety is sublime. And God never denies his attributes in those who are his light in the world. They shine like the stars in the cosmos, "innocent . . . [and] without blemish in the midst of a crooked and perverse generation" (Phil 2:15), and even their anxiety, if God allows it, bears the marks of their divine destiny.